JAGUAR
Victory '90

THE STORY OF THE 1990 LE MANS RACE

KEN WELLS

KIMBERLEY

Haynes

A KIMBERLEY Motor Sport Book

First published 1990

Published by:
Haynes Publishing Group,
Sparkford, Nr. Yeovil,
Somerset BA22 7JJ, England.

Haynes Publications Inc.,
861 Lawrence Drive,
Newbury Park,
California 91320, USA.

Produced for William Kimberley Ltd by:
Prancing Tortoise Publications,
4 Highfield Rise,
Althorne,
Essex CM3 6DN, England.

Front cover illustration by
Rosemary Hutchings.

The photographs in this book have been
supplied by: John Allen, Lyn Chalk,
Daytona International Speedway,
Gordon Dawkins, Phil Johnson, Ron
Major, W H Murenbeeld, Alan Stacey,
Jim Stanton, Ken Wells and
Zoom Photographic.

British Library Cataloguing in
Publication Data

Wells, Ken *1949 –*
Jaguar
1. Jaguar Cars
I. Title
629, 222

ISBN 0–94613–267–4

Library of Congress Catalog Card
Number: 90–84256

Printed in England by:
J. H. Haynes & Co Ltd

Designed by:
RD Illustrations, West Kingsdown,
Kent.

Typesetting by:
Fleetlines, Southend-on-Sea, Essex.

Artwork/Repro:
Hilo Offset, Colchester, Essex.

CONTENTS

THE PHANTOM OF THE OPERA

It was Wednesday lunchtime, the day before practice began for this year's Daytona 24 Hours. The last moments of tranquillity before the rigours of a long weekend were quietly ebbing away.

Up on the beach where in days gone by many a hero had raced his name into the history books, a cool wind whipped up little white tops on a slate grey sea. Just offshore a couple of fishing boats bobbed and fell with the waves as they made their way from the distant horizon to break on the wide and sandy shore. It was cool, it was overcast, there being no sign of the heat the weekend would bring with it both on and off the track.

Over at the town's airport, immediately beyond the back straight, the racers were coming to town. Some people were looking for rental cars, others for accommodation. Some people were looking for other people. It had a tantalising sort of chaos about it, the air full of optimism and anticipation as the first event of the new season grew ever closer, the ongoing question mark over the possibility of their being no Le Mans this year, therefore projecting this to be the premier 24 Hours race of 1990, only adding to the situation. Arriving as they were from all corners of the globe, with many of those present not having seen each other since the last races of the eighties, today was a time to renew old friendships, tomorrow the time to renew old rivalrys.

There was nothing to do except wait, watch some television, maybe do a few newspaper crossword puzzles and quizzes, even if they were a couple of days old. Monday's edition of the 'Miami Tribune' had asked the question: Who said 'The Opera Isn't Over Until The Fat Lady Sings'? The answer: Dick Motta. Before the week was out although few would be able to recall the name of the former Washington Bullets coach, subconsciously or otherwise his immortal line would forever be burned into their memories. Especially if you had anything to do with the Jags.

The TWR Castrol Jaguars were out for revenge. Debut winners in 1988, last year they had lost out to Porsche by only 87 seconds after twenty-four gruelling hours, Jim Busby's factory favoured Miller/BFGoodrich 962 taking the accolades in the closest finish in the history of Daytona's classic race. And although the team had recovered to record three IMSA wins during the course of the year, including the last two races of an eventful season, that narrow defeat still rankled. There was no doubt about it: TWR were out for revenge.

So it was something of a surprise when only two cars were entered instead of their customary three. There again, it only takes one to win. Both were powered by the familiar six litre V12 rather than the new turbo engine which had suffered a few hits and plenty of misses since being introduced midway through '89, especially the European version. Yet rather than reverting to 'Old Faithful' it was more a case of the new faithful, their being so many revisions incorporated into the cars since the corresponding meeting last year that they had been redesignated appropriately enough as XJR12s.

Most obvious of the changes was the use of Goodyear tyres mounted on BBS rims, thereby giving them a wholly more splendid and purposeful appearance, especially when the rear spats were off.

The Opera Isn't Over Until The Fat Lady Sings.

Jan Lammers and a Jaguar V12 – the perfect combination.

JAN LAMMERS (JAGUAR #61): "Physically, the race is very hard. You notice it most in your hands and thumbs, from gripping the steering wheel, and in your arms and neck. . . . A race like this is somewhat like life. You are judged by the last one per cent of it and you spend ninety-nine per cent getting there."

OSCAR LARRAURI (PORSCHE #3): "I don't know what happened. I went to pass a Camel Lights car and suddenly I could no longer control the car. The back end wiggled and then, I don't know, I flip over one time, two times and then – BOOM – the car went over sliding on it's top. I kept waiting for it to stop. I'm sliding upside down saying 'stop, please stop' but it wouldn't."

DAN GURNEY (TOYOTA TEAM): "Winning the pole doesn't amount to a hill of beans. We're tricking the other guys into going for it!"

GEOFF BRABHAM (NISSAN #83/84): "I am kind of disappointed (in not sitting on the pole) but it's difficult trying to get a clear lap in this situation. You're out there praying for a clear lap with the softest tyres you've got and it comes to nothing more than a crap shoot."

BOB WOLLEK (PORSCHE #86): "It was just the normal job. . . ."

Allied to these were subtle suspension changes and modifications to the bodywork, notably the addition of NACA ducts in the nose, thereby deleting the need for small oval ones immediately beneath the headlamps. At the very rear the angled exhaust tail pipes of twelve months ago gave way to a pair of straight mufflers which looked for all the world like a pair of howitzers. Maybe they were.

Scheduled to drive chassis –388/Car #61 were regular TWR campaigners Jan Lammers, Davy Jones and Andy Wallace while in the other car, race number #60 being chassis –288 and therefore built around the winning tub from 1988, were the familiar smiling faces of John Nielsen and Price Cobb and also Martin Brundle. Having recently resigned his seat in the Brabham F.1. team, thereby turning his back on Grand Prix racing for a second time, the 1988 World Sports-Prototype champion was a welcome retournee to the TWR fold still recoiling from the late defection of Eddie Cheever who had elected at the eleventh hour to go IndyCar racing instead. Martin had planned to do Daytona, now he would stay for the whole season.

In their previous visits Jaguar had pulled out all the stops and tried for pole position despite 'only' having atmospheric engines, missing out narrowly on both occasions. This time, especially with the battle for the top slots settled by a Thursday afternoon free-for-all rather than the traditional Daytona custom of single car qualifying, TWR decided not to play that particular game and happily filled the fifth row of the two-by-two grid, Jaguar #60 being half a second down on last year, the other V12 a further 1.3 seconds in arrears as the Indiana based outfit concentrated on their race set-up.

Instead, qualifying was all about turbos and big boost engines. It was also about the enormous accident which befell Oscar Larrauri. Flat out through Turn Four, 'Popi' had already eclipsed Sarel van der Merwe's all-time track record (set in 1985 aboard a Lola Corvette) and was on another flyer when he came across a Camel Lights car high on the banking. Electing to dive down low rather than unsettle the car by quickly backing off the pace, as he did so the right rear Yokohama exploded, spinning the Brun 962 around and flipping it onto its roof.

Fortunately, the Thompson built chassis took the strain and when the Torno supported car finally came to a halt, despite having the front roll over bar depressed and his helmet ground down by the tarmac the shaken Larrauri was miraculously unhurt although the experience probably did add some more grey hairs to his neatly cropped salt'n'pepper locks. Too badly damaged for immediate repair, the wreck was eventually returned to Thompson's to

be dealt with after the Silverstone WSPC encounter many weeks later.

For a while it looked as if the race would have a pole position car *in absentia* but those who thought that way reckoned without Bob Wollek. Hurtling his Texaco Havoline 962 around in a wonderful display of controlled aggression 'Brilliant Bob' clipped a full second off the lap record to leave the new mark at 1m37.832 seconds, an average speed of 131 miles per hour down to the third decimal place. 'Super Van', for his part, was no more than slightly nonplussed at the loss of his piece of history by virtue of the fact that he was partnering Wollek and Dominic Dobson in Bruce Leven's Bayside Racing black beauty.

Locked in alongside the Porsche (chassis 962-139) on the front row was Geoff Brabham, the double IMSA champion unable to better 1m37.883 in the omnipotent Nissan Performance Technology (formerly Electramotive) ZXT, number #84. Sharing the driving duties on a pair of entries with Chip Robinson, Derek Daly and Bob Earl, the second 'works' Nissan lined up third, there being no sign yet of the much anticipated replacement NPT90.

A third Nissan, one of last year's cars now earning its keep in the possesion of defending race champions Busby Racing, lined up on Row Three, Mauro Baldi taking time out from his Mercedes WSPC duties to share the multi-coloured car with John Paul Jr. and Kevin Cogan, the latter keen to forget *that* accident at the 1989 Indy 500. Fortunately for him, Daytona does not have an outer pitlane wall so he could hardly repeat it even if he wanted to.

Sandwiched between the Nissans were two more Porsches, both of which were utilising Group C style undertrays rather than the previously conventional IMSA type and thereby subject to a 100 pounds weight penalty. Fourth was the Joest entry (962–011, the 1989 Dijon WSPC winner) for Frank Jelinski, Henri Pescarolo and renta-driver Jean-Louis Ricci slightly ahead of the homegrown Rob Dyson who sported a brand new car, chassis 962-148, for himself and the very talented driving team of Vern Schuppan, James Weaver and rising IndyCar star Scott Pruett. Not that such a line up is of much use if the car owner sticks it in the boonies after a few laps. . . .

Seventh on the grid came Jochen Dauer's Thompson chassised 962, 1987 WSPC champion Raul Boesel lined up to do the event with IndyCar superstar 'Little Al' Unser, twice a former winner, and his young cousin Robby (son of Uncle Bobby) who was having his first taste of something so big and bold. Alongside sat six litres of Spice Chevy V8 pedalled by Mister Kline, Signor Jourdain and Matsushita-san, their National Panasonic liveried SE90C edging out Jaguar as top of the atmospheric stakes.

With the loss of the Torno machine, the GTP class was down to only fifteen cars, next up being Dan Gurneys Eagle Toyota. Powered by a highly strung 2.1 litre turbo four, everyone expected the Santa Ana machine to be fast yet fragile and so it would prove. The other four were all Porsches, the old ex-Dyson DSR car, the almost new Shapiro/Alucraft entry of Rene Herzog (who also practiced his Ford Probe V8 with no serious intention of racing it), the newish Momo/Gebhardt example and the positively ancient Wynn's version. Fritz Gebhardt also brought along one of his own chassies fitted with an Audi engine from the Trans-Am programme. It was only seen briefly.

All of the latter may have been out of the limelight during qualifying but with the twists of fortune which could be expected in a full lap of the sundial, plus drivers the calibre of Derek Bell and Hans Stuck, Hurley Haywood and Stanley Dickens, none could be overlooked for a decent result. Indeed, triple winner Bell had gone on record to say that his Momo machine was the best Porsche he had ever driven at Daytona, bar none. On that basis any of them were capable of springing a surprise or two. Unfortunately, the one reserved for 'Dinger' would shock himself more than the opposition.

The DSR, Alucraft and Wynn's entries all featured air cooled flat-sixes with single turbos, the other Porsches benefitting from having water cooled versions with twin turbochargers. All were three litres, the same as the Nissans.

Yet despite the optimism of the lower ranks any betting man would be placing his money further up the grid. The top Porsches all seemed to be in with a more than reasonable chance while after their impressive front running display last year (in their long distance debut) the Nissans could not be discounted. And all the while the Jaguar drivers just went about their business, post qualifying conversations with the likes of Andy Wallace oozing unprecedented confidence where a 'we will have to wait and see' would normally suffice. Did they know something the rest of the world didn't?

The answer to that and all the other questions would be known by 3.30 on Sunday afternoon but before then so many things could and would happen, the good, the bad and the downright calamitous. . . .

As the cars sped into view and under the starter's flag Bob Wollek pulled low and led into the first turn, the rest of the field stringing out behind his Porsche as he headed towards the infield. Taking the sweeps and curves with consummate grace, by the time the Texaco Star reached the West Banking its advantage was a full one hundred yards and moving out.

Down the back straightaway for the first time they went, the fastest of this multi-hued ribbon of speed topping 200 miles an hour before going hard on the brakes, flicking left then right, a quick jab of throttle, right then left, and accelerating hard and high towards the unforgiving wall atop the East Banking.

Riding it the full 180-degrees all the way back to the Start/Finish line Bob was two hundred yards clear as he completed Lap One, Jelinski showing in third to split the Nissans, Unser Jr. next up followed by the Jaguars. Ninth was Rob Dyson pedalling his brand new 962 but such glory would be shortlived, the car due to come to rest with its rear end atop two layers of armco barrier after only six laps when its owner managed to outmanoeuvre himself with disasterous consequences. There would be no race for James Weaver or Vern Schuppan although Scott Pruett took time out to transfer his services to former mentor Jack Roush who was attempting to win the IMSA GTO category for an incredible sixth consecutive year.

By the time the embarrassed Dyson started the long walk home the race had a new leader, Jelinski taking second from Bob Earl at the chicane on Lap 2 then making up a lot of ground to reel in Wollek on the run down past the grandstands three laps later. Frank was on a charge.

The Busby Nissan was not. Slipping backwards down the order at an alarming rate, with only a quarter of an hour gone it had already dropped from fifth to tenth, the next fifteen minutes seeing it lose four more places. The suspension which had been removed to facilitate a post-Warm Up engine change (completed only minutes before the start) was not performing as required and the consequent oversteer proving difficult for John Paul Jr. to live with. Although this would later be adjusted to form a more competitive set-up, it was the beginning of the end for the team which had won in such fine style twelve months ago.

Two Porsches led a brace of Nissans followed closely by the pair of Jaguars. With half an hour gone already they were well amongst the backmarkers, one Nissan and a Jaguar going high to the right of a lonely 911 as it thundered down the back stretch, the other XJR going low and left, all four of them side-by-side inches apart for a few tantalising seconds as nobody gave any thought to backing off, there still being a long race to run. Unable to make it five wide,

'Little Al' kept a watching brief a few lengths behind. It was getting hectic out there.

Back in the pits the service crews awaited the first of what would become a regular chore of pitstops until nigh on this time tomorrow. First of the leaders to seek replenishment and rubber was Wollek, his place behind the wheel of Porsche #86 taken by van der Merwe. With the barest minimum of time lost soon the South African found himself hurtling down pitlane into the fray, ready to take up the cudgels where Bob had left off.

Soon afterwards Nissan #84 arrived, not that things turned out to be so straight forward for the quasi-Japanese outfit. During refuelling a fuel union broke, the ensuing fire doing enough damage to put the car out of contention. The team had always planned to withdraw one of their charges after about an hour so as to concentrate their efforts on the other and the fire had made the decision for them.

Cleaned up and checked over, after a long delay Nissan #84 would spend some time scrubbing in tyres for its sister car before being pushed away. It would then reappear during the night for a few hours. Just after dawn broke so did its engine.

Next in was Jelinski, his very impressive opening stint lasting just short of an hour. Handing over to Pescarolo, a fairly leisurely pitstop saw the Joest 962 rejoin just as the Leven/Texaco car swept by into the lead. Already up to pace whereas 'Pepsi Cola' had to build warmth into his tyres and rhythm into his driving, by the end of the lap 'Super Van' had opened up a crucial margin between them.

It lasted for all of eight minutes. Determined to maintain his advantage, while negotiating heavy traffic in the infield Sarel cut between two cars he was attempting to pass, a GTO Camaro to the left, a Camel Lights slightly ahead to the right, and hit the Chevy a glancing blow. The result was a deflated tyre, damaged bodywork and deranged rear wing. As he hobbled back to the pits at much reduced pace Pescarolo sped on by, the hard work of retaking the lead having been done for him.

Five minutes later and it was undone, the Joest 962 spinning to a halt on the infield grass as the left rear suspension buckled beneath it. Over an hour would be lost rectifying the fault, alas to no avail when the engine quit in mid evening to end a gallant run which had promised much yet delivered little.

As a result of all this chaos, without upping the pace of their attack Jaguar found themselves in the lead. The game plan had been to pick a race pace and stick to it, hopefully to be in a position to challenge for the win come breakfast time on Sunday. By keeping out of mischief they now found themselves at the front twelve hours too early!

The trick would be how to stay there. Threatened by Nissan #83 which sometimes managed to get ahead as the race ebbed and flowed due to back-markers and pitstops – everyone else at least half a lap in arrears – as two then three hours came and went the inevitable arrival of sundown was greeted by a pair of gorgeous Castrol V12s putting on a magnificent high speed show as they lapped in tandem, frequently no more than a few feet apart, often running side-by-side on the banking as if on a high speed demonstration run. Which, of course, they were.

While the Jags went on their merry way into the night things were not so good at the far end of pitlane, chez Bayside. Having got back into the swing of things following van der Merwe's little escapade, matters had taken another turn for the worse soon afterwards when an oil union broke, dropping the black car out of the top twelve. Although (according to a team spokesman) the bit which caused the grief retailed at only US$5.59 it would cost them dearly, the nine laps lost in effecting a repair crucial in the long run, the full extent of which would only become apparent on Sunday afternoon.

Not destined to be around at the finish was Spice #33, the team's progress board telling its own story by simply stating 'Kline Meets Mazda' there then being an ominous gap before the final comment 'And Loses'. Pushed hard into the armco by a wayward RX–7, Jeff was very fortunate to escape injury, the severity of the incident enough to write-off a newly purchased monocoque. The National Panasonic liveried device had been seventh when the Mazda – and disaster – struck.

Three hours later Derek Bell suffered an even more frightening fate. In an incident very reminiscent to that which had befallen Larrauri a few days earlier, an exploding tyre put the Moretti/Momo 962 onto its roof at the exit of Turn Four, the sparks emanating from carbon fibre and metal being worn away at high speed lighting up the night sky as the remains of the red'n'yellow Porsche slid to a halt just prior to the pitlane entrance, its driver soaked in spilt fuel. Sixth at the time, the car having survived a couple of wild spins in the early going, there would be no addition to the trophy cabinet this time for 'Dinger', a cut lip his only souvenir of a disappointing weekend with its dramatic finale.

Back on pitlane something stirred.

Coming as it did just before quarter distance, as six hours passed into history the leader board showed that this was fast becoming a three horse race, only the surviving 'works' NPTI Nissan able to stay with the Jaguars. The only other vehicle which could have been considered a direct threat was the Dauer car, Boesel and the Unsers one lap adrift and keen to erase the embarrassment of having been arrested on Thursday evening for some high speed frolics on a local highway. Fifth was the Gurney Toyota, four laps further in arrears, then the Busby Nissan, the Alucraft 962 of 'Stucky' & Co. and the Wynn's Porsche. A dozen laps down, the Texaco Star shone dimly in ninth just one place ahead of a Mercury Cougar which led the GTO class and the rest, rounding out the top ten.

The Nissan was certainly making a fight of it. Never letting the Castrol cars out of its sight, the XJRs slower around the infield but quicker on the straights, TWR determined not to be harried into over-stretching themselves. Yet in a game of thrust and parry where races are won as much by tactics as speed, the Jaguars may have been the cats but, for sure, the Nissan was no mouse. More a hound.

And with an hour of Saturday left the Nissan moved ahead, both Jaguars losing a little time in the run up to midnight, the #60 car sustaining a puncture which dropped it temporarily to fourth, while the erstwhile leader, Castrol #61, had a replacement tail fitted when its rear lights stopped working.

Others wished their problems were so simple. Soon afterwards Dauer lost two hours with transmission difficulties while the Gurney Toyota was also becoming a more familiar sight in the pits than on the track due to overheating dramas. Although the Porsche would battle on until sunrise when finally thwarted by engine problems, the 'other' Japanese car was about to fade away, its chances having evaporated with its coolant.

As Saturday night turned into Sunday morning the Nissan still tended to hold a slight advantage, the Jaguars usually lined up mere seconds behind, these three now a full seven laps clear of the Busby ZXT which had inherited fourth from Dauer, the fast recovering Texaco Porsche another four laps back and just about to move ahead of the Alucraft version for fifth. Seventh, still leading the GTO category, came the thundering red Cougar.

Onwards they charged into the night. Whereas everybody else seemed to be facing one major calamity after another the front three went on their way in apparent harmony, only the smallest of delays hindering their progress. If this continued, the race would be won on the vagaries of dealing with traffic and the slickness of pitstops. As if to stress the point, with ten hours run the Nissan handed first position back to Jaguar for no other reason than the delay caused in trying to shut a door.

All across the infield camp fires were now burning bright, a wild and fun place to be as revellers mixed the serious business of party time with pondering slightly less significant matters such as the meaning of life and the outcome of the race, not necessarily in that order. With still such a long way to go, motor racing at its best, especially endurance events, is ideally suited to barrack room lawyers and armchair pundits, the result unsure right up until the chequered flag.

Over in the Press Room, it was much the same. Without the partying. As a hard core from the media continued to monitor what was happening on a closed circuit television screen, the less committed having gone off to various freebie junkets and/or to bed, some busied themselves filing their reports as events unravelled in front of them, their concentration stretched to the limit by one of their number who persisted in expounding his personal theories out loud to anyone who would listen, and everyone who wouldn't. Him apart, only the soft mutterings of French and German, Japanese and American, mixing with a constant dull thud of plastic keys on electronic keyboards, could be heard.

Back on pitlane something stirred. At 1.48am the 'works' Nissan could be seen cruising down on the apron and as it glided to a stop beneath the pale yellow lights off came the rear cover. A wisp of smoke curled away on the night air.

For a while it stood there unattended and alone, both doors hinged high into the air as if in surrender. A few moments later the crew pushed their charge behind the wall, the engine having suffered a major malfunction. Although it would make a brief reappearance, never again would a 'works' Nissan be a threat to Jaguar in Superbowl'90.

Instead it was the privateer Busby version which took up the challenge, striving to get on terms but not for long. Less than three hours later in the latest twist of events which had seen more dramas than a whole host of soap operas it too suffered terminal engine damage and was entered into oblivion.

The opposition was crumbling. One by one, all of those who would deny Jaguar a repeat of their 1988 success had hit major problems whereas for the XJR12s their constant lap after constant lap routine had continued virtually interrupted. Indeed, the nearest they had come to disaster was a short time earlier when Martin Brundle had exited the pits only to drive straight into the armco barrier on cold tyres, thereby requiring an extra stop to replace the nosecone. The motor racing equivelent of shooting oneself in the foot, fortunately the most significant effect of the contretemps was to allow Jaguar #61 to eke out its advantage to a full two laps.

As the sun began appearing in earnest over the East Banking it was the Texaco car which now found itself in third place with less than nine hours to go. Theirs had been a mighty effort to get back on terms with the leaders yet with a fifteen lap deficit on the second placed car (they had also lost some time when a front brake duct came lose) all they could realistically hope for was something to

strike down both Coventry machines in short order and as the warm early rays began to lift everyone's spirits that seemed very unlikely.

Fourth was the Alucraft 962, another nine laps back having been delayed by valve train problems, the two Cougars next, split only by the much delayed Wynn's Porsche. Nobody else was within two hours driving time of the XJRs. To all intents and purposes, for many observers the result seemed pretty much a forgone conclusion, the race all over bar the shouting.

In the Jaguar pit there was an air of quiet confidence, knowing as they did that even if both cars were to be parked for thirty minutes they could still resume holding the first two places. Theirs was not one shot at winning but two. As the pair of red, white and green machines reeled off lap after lap, apparently unruffled and obviously unhurried, their advantage was so huge it was almost embarrassing. Much as with the San Francisco 49-ers against the Denver Broncos the previous weekend, this was no contest, this was annihilation.

But with the equivelent of almost half a season of WSPC racing still to go before the chequered flag appeared, the fat lady had yet to complete her scales let alone sing the song.

By nine o'clock the pair could be seen once again in tandem as if practicing a formation finish, the sight and sound of the battle stained chariots in the fresh morning air a tonic to all but those who chased in vain. After the close run things of the past two years it was all so easy.

There was not much else to do but await the outcome, a couple of TWR crew men busying themselves finishing

Driven by Raul Boesel with Robby and 'Little Al' Unser, for a long time the Dauer 962 was the leading Porsche only to be thwarted by gearbox problems and then a broken engine.

off repairs to the nosecone damaged in Brundle's earlier indescretion. It occupied the mind, it took up time, as the clock ticked ever on.

After the rigours of a night of partying the lack of fight for the lead made it easy for some of the less committed gathered amidst the motor homes and rental trucks to take only a passing interest in on-track affairs.

Almost unnoticed by all but those with their minds firmly on the race track, the second placed Jaguar had been remorselessly catching the leader, pulling up to just one lap in arrears a little before nine o'clock, unlapping itself less than an hour and a quarter later. With five hours to go they were just over one minute apart.

Jaguar #61 had built up its lead not so much by outright speed but stealth, having spent less time in the pits than its sister car which, lap for lap, had been driven harder and faster. Now the Brundle/Cobb/Nielsen machine was making up lost ground.

At first onlookers thought the Jones/Lammers/Wallace combo were taking it easy, not willing to be pushed into going too fast even by their team mates. But as the gap diminished it became more and more obvious that such assumptions were incorrect. Jaguar #61 was in trouble.

11

84
BOSCH
GOODYEAR
NISSAN
performance
technology, inc.
CIBA-
GEIGY
NISSAN

DEREK BELL (PORSCHE #30): "I was flat out running the banking when something broke in the rear. It skidded on and on and on. I hit nothing but I put on the extinguisher because I was afraid of a possible fire. I was still upside down and the engine was on. I switched it off but was soaked in fuel and started to pass out from the fumes. I could not get out through the windscreen. I was looking up the road and hearing the cars go by. I passed out. It was like a dream. I remember having nightmares. . . . In twenty years I have never crashed out of a race but I have now!"

DAN GURNEY (TOYOTA TEAM): "We cleaned out the radiators really well, added some water, fuelled it, put on a new windshield and gave it a shave and a haircut."

JIM BUSBY (NISSAN #67): "It could be a long night. I've got one driver who runs 1.42s and passes everything in sight and two others that run in the 1.46 to 1.50 range. We are not being consistent and it's costing us."

JOHN HOTCHKIS Sr. (PORSCHE #10): "The Gods of Racing haven't smiled on us at all. . ."

GEOFF BRABHAM (NISSAN #83/84): "It's tough. I already knew that but I needed reminding. When the race was nine hours old it really sunk in as to what incredible effort and luck has to go into a race like this. It's mind boggling!"

JAN LAMMERS (JAGUAR #61): "I had no problems with my night shift. It was very boring but it's worth it."

Nissan came and saw but failed to conquer.

The Wynn's 962; last home of the GTP cars in sixth place.

Jack Roush notched an amazing sixth consecutive GTO-class win thanks to Robby Gordon, Calvin Fish and Lyn St.James.

During the night it had suffered from a sudden sharp rise in water temperature. With the help of those long, cool hours of darkness things had soon gotten back to normal. Now, as the hot sun rose in the morning sky so did the figures being registered inside the cramped confines of the leading cockpit, the water temperature guage about to hit the red. And with it a strange quietness came over the Jaguar contingent, the bouyant expectancy of a few short hours ago now muted. With less than five hours to go, the fat lady might be starting to sing but as far as Jaguar were concerned she was decidedly off key. . . .

Four times in the first half of the eleventh hour of the day TWR's No.#61 stopped for coolant, clouds of steam rising high into the clear blue sky as hot water was added to an even hotter engine, much of the liquid evaporating before it ever reached its supposed destination.

Things were getting desperate. They sacrificed the crew coffee-making machine to the cause, this ready source of heated water the best assurance anyone had of avoiding a cracked cylinder head, that being the likely fate if cold water were used. They also sent the car out minus its rear tail section, the draught created over the glowing V12 doing nothing for the aerodynamic equation but wonders for the temperature readings. By the time the faraway clocks in old Daytona town struck high noon things were coming under control. Or so they hoped.

Actually, it was more as if the evil spirits had tired of Jaguar #61 and decided to move along to have some fun with what was now the new leader. Twenty minutes into the afternoon session and it was Jaguar #60's turn to find itself in trouble. The ghoulies and ghosties, flibbertigibbets and phantoms were coming out to play. And how.

A routine brake disc and pad change turned into a near disaster, hot pads proving reluctant to be removed, the car at a standstill for well over eight minutes. Racing cars are only cooled by moving, the rush of air through those great orifices doing the job (hopefully) as they speed on their way. Standing still does them no favours whatsoever and so it proved in this instance. As if to emulate what had gone before, twice within the next half an hour Jaguar #60 would need replenishment of its water reservoir, handing the lead back to its team mates once again. Hubble, bubble, boil and trouble.

Time was running out and so was their lead. In just over an hour the Texaco Star had managed to reduce the deficit from sixteen laps to ten. The fastest car on the course, any further difficulties for the Jags and the race could be in for a dramatic finish after all. Encouraged at the prospect, Wollek, Dobson and van der Merwe piled on the pressure.

And it was beginning to show. Not so much on the track but in the Castrol Jaguar enclave. The daytime temperature may have been soaring to record highs but thereabouts everyone was breaking out in a cold sweat as the very real prospect of a last gasp defeat loomed ever larger and more possible.

Price Cobb, for one, was down and almost out. Suffering from heat exhaustion he could be seen stretched out flat on his back on a table, the sponsor-approved red'n'white green stemmed carnations at his side wilting in the sun yet still looking to have more zest left in them than the moustachioed Colorado based Texan. Close by, Sir John Egan appeared worried and tight lipped, the furrowed brow of Jaguar USA chief Graham Whitehead getting ever deeper.

Even the usually ebullient John Gardella from Castrol was more subdued than normal. There was also the sight of Tom Walkinshaw, Mister Cool himself, actually *running* around marshalling his troops for the final assault. Nobody could remember seeing the Scot break into a trot before, let alone a gallop. Things really were getting serious.

Down pitlane at the home of Leven/ Texaco they knew, just as everyone else did, that there was nothing to say that the problems with the Jaguars might not become terminal. Two hours from the end and the black Porsche had chipped another lap from the deficit, enough to prove their determination and own good health, not sufficient to cause any undue concern to TWR unless things got worse.

Bruce Leven's team were wishing and hoping on their Texaco Star, Tom Walkinshaw's equipe thinking and praying for the ninth life of their Castrol Cats. As the race entered its final hour the Porsche charged on, the XJRs attempting to run fast enough not to be caught yet not so quickly as to add to their troubles, track speed obviously a determining factor regarding their cooling problems. It was a terrible dilemma and one which would have been considerably worse if it had not been for the nine laps Porsche #86 had lost replacing that cheap oil union so many long and frustrating hours ago. Nine laps down with less than sixty minutes to go, another motor racing 'if only' looked set to enter the annals of legend and folklore.

And so it was. The leading car slowed even further in the final period but still finished six laps in front of the Porsche. Wollek & Co. did, however, almost catch the second placed Jaguar which needed three more stops for coolant to come home only a scant two laps ahead of the German machine. It had probably taken Jaguar over $250,000 to win the Daytona 24 Hours. It had taken Porsche less than six bucks to lose it.

Fourth, a whopping fifty-one laps behind the Texaco Porsche came the Alucraft 962, itself fifteen laps ahead of the GTO winning Mercury Cougar. Jack Roush had achieved his dream of a sixth straight class win although not without its own dramas, his leading car stopping with a broken driveshaft during the last half an hour. Fortunately for him the team's second effort was there to take over when necessary. And just to make absolutely certain next up

was a Roush Capri V8.

Sixth was the Wynn's Porsche, its classification of fifth in class flattering to deceive by virtue of the fact it was also last of the GTP runners, all the rest having succumbed along the way. The ESCO Argo won Camel Lights after a steady run, another Mazda engined device in the form of the Uria RX–7 doing the honours in GTU.

As a very happy Jan Lammers brought Castrol Jaguar #61 across the finish line a great cheer went up from all those who had held their cumulative breath for so long, the huge outpouring of emotion as much in relief as ecstacy. The T-shirts they had brought with them bearing the legend 'Castrol Jaguar – 1990 Daytona 24 Hours Winners' would not be wasted after all.

Two years ago many of those same people had also been present when TWR had gone to America and won the race at the first time of asking. It had then gone on to claim the greatest sports car racing prize of all at Le Mans a few months later.

Last year, having looked so formidable for a very long time they had finally succumbed to the fates and lost out in the final analysis, a similar despair ultimately dogging their efforts in France as well.

Now, in the golden glow of a setting sun, once again the mighty V12 had powered its way into Victory Lane thereby raising the question as to whether they could make history repeat itself and once again pull off the double. The answer would be known a mere nineteen weeks later, subject to the FISA versus ACO conflict being resolved, of course.

But that was all to the future. Today had been a superb victory in its own right, one underlined by the fact that despite those late dramas the winners had put up a new record distance for the event at 2,709 miles. The second placed car also exceeded the old mark.

As the sound of the last engines died away and the final hurrahs drifted on a freshening breeze you would swear you could have heard a fat lady singing for all she was worth. . . .

With its water temperature guage as high as the banking, Jaguar #61 ran for a while without its rear decking in an attempt to cool things down. It worked.

Timed to perfection.

To the winners the spoils.

DAYTONA DITTIES

The first ever major sports car race at Daytona was in 1962, Dan Gurney winning the 3-Hours event in his Lotus 19. Having built up a sizeable advantage early on, it was sudden drama when the engine seized a few minutes before the end as Phil Hill closed rapidly in his Ferrari. Required by the rules to cross the finishing line under its own power, Dan waited patiently high up on the banking until the clock struck the top of the hour and then let the Lotus roll home down the slope on the starter motor!

Winners of the first Daytona 24, in 1966, were Ken Miles and Lloyd Ruby in a Ford GT. Coincidentally, they had also been the winners of the previous year's race, the last of the early series with a duration of three hours.

One of endurance racing's biggest upsets occurred at Daytona in 1969 when the battered Lola Chevy of Mark Donohue and Chuck Parsons outlasted all the top runners to win by a whopping 32 laps. With another of the T70s in second place it was the best ever result for one of Eric Broadley's most famous creations.

Nowadays, the 24 Hours uses three of Daytonas four banked turns, each of which is 31-degrees. This compares mightily with those of Indianapolis which are a 'mere' 9-degrees. Even the Daytona start/finish line is 18-degrees above horizontal!

Only five drivers have won all three endurance classics i.e. the Daytona 24 Hours, the Sebring 12 Hours and the Le Mans 24 Hours. They are A.J.Foyt, Hurley Haywood, Al Holbert, Hans Hermann and Jackie Oliver. Jacky Ickx did win at Daytona in 1972 but unfortunately for him that year the event only lasted six hours due to the Oil Crisis.

Nobody has ever won all three classics in the same year. Al Holbert has come nearest to doing the triple, winning both the Daytona and Le Mans races in 1987 and coming second at Sebring after having led for ten hours before being delayed by turbo problems. He eventually lost out by less than three laps.

French born Spice-Buick driver Ferdinand de Lesseps is the great, great grandson of the man who not only was instrumental in constructing both the Suez and Panama Canals but also gave the dedication speech for the Statue of Liberty.

One of the world's strangest ever 24 Hours races was that which took place in 1928 at Indianapolis. There were only two cars!

At the previous year's London Motor Show, Stutz boss Fred Moskovics said he would be delighted to take on Rolls-Royce to determine whose was the best car in the world. R-R were typically unimpressed so a Frenchman named Charles T Weymann offered his Hispano Suiza instead. As both were regarded as the fastest cars of their respective continents at that time it seemed like the ideal match race, the Hispano H6 very advanced but the Stutz Black Hawk possibly more refined.

Weymann won after the Stutz dropped a valve in the twentieth hour, its driver Tom Rooney having over strained early on it in a vain effort to build an advantage. The wager between the two owners on the outcome was a princely $25–00!

Robbie Gordon, GTO class winner and desert racing ace, had to pay $120 for a taxi ride from Orlando Airport when he accepted Jack Roush's invitation to test for the team at Sebring a few months prior to the race. Being under 21-years old at the time he was too young to hire a car.

Daytona was his very first car race of any description on a paved track. So new to the game was he that when he arrived at the track to sign-on he didn't even have a full racing licence!

The GTU class winning Mazda RX–7 was no stranger to Victory Lane. Four times in the last five years its owner 'Famous' Amos Johnson had done the trick in the very same car. On this occasion he leased it out to Pete Uria who promptly made it five from six to score his first IMSA success. For his part, Johnson helped drive the Downing RX–7 to second in GTO.

Kennedy Space Center is less than an hour's drive south of Daytona and is well worth a visit. Amongst the attractions are a couple of excellent bus tours of the 84,000 acre facility. They are operated by a company called TW Recreational Services, Inc. Is there nothing that man doesn't have a stake in. . . .

Also to be seen at the Kennedy Space Center is a Gemini rocket wearing a FiA sticker. The same type as used to take the likes of John Glenn into space, could this be the ultimate fate for those who upset the inhabitants of the Place de la Concorde? I think we should be told. . . .

Porsche press notes at Daytona stated that Stanley Dickens was related to the famous by virtue of the fact that his (quote) grandfather's grandfather's father's brother was Charles Dickens (unquote). Yet it categorically failed to mention that he won the 1989 Le Mans 24 Hours. It's all Oliver Twist to me!

Endeavouring to glean as much information as possible, early in the week before things got really busy your intrepid reporter approached a guy at one of the tyre companies as he went about his business of putting rubber on rims.

"How many tyres would you use here this week?" I asked in my best English accent. "Aw, 'bout four thousan' I guess" came back the reply, my new found friend obviously presuming I meant y'all rather than just his specific company.

Undeterred, I continued the line of questioning, commenting that it seemed like a lot. He put me firmly in my place. "If this were Sebring we'd use twelve thousan' coz that's rougher than a corn cob."

"So this is soft on tyres?" I continued.

The reply was short and sweet. "Nah, Firestone."

BACK TO THE FUTURE

The lead up to the 58th Grand Prix d'Endurance de Vingt-Quatre Heures du Mans was, to say the least, unusual. Three of the four WSPC races preceding it were won by a team who had no intention of going to France if the event was outside the championship, which it was. The other saw victory go to a team which would enter cars totally different from those with which they now competed in the WSPC. . . .

Mercedes – as they now simply wished to be known rather than the Sauber Mercedes of ages past – had started off the year the way they meant to go on; entering two cars in the opening rounds at Suzuka and Monza and duly coming home first and second in both. Having won all but a single race they contested last year, all in all it could have been deemed as a bit like watching yet another re-run of 'The Magnificent Seven'; still entertaining but very familiar.

Actually, it was more a case of 'The Great Escape'. With only a few hundred yards of the new season gone their chances of success looked slim, at best. Having comprehensively damaged the new Sauber built carbon fibre C11 in practice when he went too fast too soon on cold tyres, Jean-Louis Schlesser had a fuel leak on the parade lap in the back-up aluminium C9 he shared with Mauro Baldi and was pushed into the pits for repairs, the race starting without him, the pack already half a lap down the road when he was finally able to begin the chase.

Meanwhile, Jochen Mass had made a tardy start from Row2 and in one of those bumping and bashing episodes which particularly seem to afflict early season races in most formulaes soon found himself spinning onto the grass, resuming in twelfth place. As with 'Schless', it was not the way it was meant to be.

From then on things could only get better and over the next three hours they duly did, the pair of Silver Arrows moving impressively up through the field to take the lead by half distance.

There was not much doubt about the result thereafter and they ran out winners by a lap over the rest. Sharing second place car with Mass was Karl Wendlinger, the 21-years old Austrian the first recipient of a new company policy of nurturing the careers of young Teutons by letting them take turns in the fourth seat. He passed his initiation test well.

In three outings there since taking over the mantle of the Silver Arrows none of the present day guardians of the legend could better second place at Monza, the evocative old circuit being restored to the WSPC calendar after a season's absence.

This time they made no mistake, Schlesser and Baldi scoring a fine debut victory – albeit one race after it should have done – for the slimline C11 designed by Leo Ress. Using the latest version of the five litre mildly turboed V8 they had campaigned with such good effect in recent seasons, albeit with heavily revised electronics, it may not have the svelte lines of its predecessor

nor even that same amazing sound, but as a racing machine it had, as feared, already proven to be more than the equal of its rivals. And just as at Suzuka three weeks earlier, the other Mercedes came second, Mass again doing the honours with Wendlinger alongside.

Oh, how Jaguar had wished for such reliability these past twelve months. When they posted the finishing order at Suzuka there was no mention of the Silk Cut cars, only Martin Brundle's late lap record to show for their troubles.

The last year had been a disaster for the Kidlington team. Deciding that the venerable V12 was being outpaced, TWR had built a turbo machine, the first of which was shown to the press at Jarama in June and raced at Brands Hatch in July. Although it managed pole position on its debut that was all the good news there really was, the project unable to get the speed and reliability within the fuel schedule necessary to put up any sort of decent challenge, a couple of fifth places not considered anything other than a huge disappointment by a team so used to winning.

Over the course of the winter TWR took many measures to rectify their slide into competitive near obscurity, one of the most significant being the switch (as did Mercedes) from Dunlop to Goodyear tyres, a move which had already worked wonders with the Daytona win. There was also a strengthening of experience in the turbo department and the recruitment of Ross Brawn from Arrows to replace the soon to depart Tony Southgate who had designed all the Walkinshaw XJRs to date but was looking for fresh fields to conquer.

Although sheared oil pump drives sidelined both Silk Cats late in the Suzuka race their overall performance was a marked and very welcome improvement on most forays of 1989. Yet while Kipling may have been content with hope where there had been despondency, Tom Walkinshaw wanted something less pragmatic and more practical. He wanted positive results.

With third and fourth at Monza he got them, Brundle and new regular partner Alain Ferte only losing second place on the last lap when their fuel ran low, their earlier progress having been hampered by 'iffy' brakes. Lammers and Wallace were not far behind.

While the Jaguars were finally getting on terms with their main rivals the same could not be said of Porsche. Entering into an amazing ninth season in the front line with the 956/962 model, the offering of the other Stuttgart manufacturer was starting to show its age, despite the factory having formally adopted Joest Racing as their 'works' team and produced a modified engine enlarged to 3.2 litres which should have, in theory at least, gotten them a lot closer to the opposition. It didn't.

The last year had been a disaster for the Kidlington team.

There in Japan, the Wollek/Jelinski machine retired after a refuelling fire while F.1. refugee Jonathan Palmer and veteran Henri Pescarolo could not better eleventh. A third car for Stanley Dickens and 'John Winter' struggled home sixteenth. It was certainly not the most auspicious of starts for the grand alliance. Things picked up slightly in Italy but a well beaten fifth and eighth are not the sort of results sports car racing's winningest marque are used to, notwithstanding the fact it has won only once in three years.

Despite not having the privelege of the new power plants, Brun took sixth in Japan, Kremer ninth at Monza. Of the other Porsche mounted regulars, RLR could not better fifteenth and seventeenth respectively while Team Davey fared even worse with its normal catalogue of woes, Obermaier not much better.

Almeras were a revelation, but only until you realised that in the Japanese race it was actually an Alpha team car which took over their entry, finishing eighth. Left to their own devices in Italy, the brothers failed to qualify. Konrad did nothing special, nor did Salamin although when hiring their name out to Nova at Suzuka they, at least, managed a surrogate tenth.

Pórsche may lack the outright pace needed for the sprint races these days but certainly not the reliability. More than half the Monza finishers were 962s while with one exception all the way from fifth to seventeenth inclusive in Japan was Porsches. That exception was the Cougar in twelfth. With a similar result in Italy the small French marque proved that they too could get the job done over the distance, albeit not as a front runner.

Nissan were expected to be right there up at the front challenging the Mercs and the Jags this time around but after the first two races they were already starting to disappoint. For the home game NISMO used a R90CJ to inherit a well beaten third for Masahiro Hasemi and Anders Olofsson when the XJRs stopped. Later, in Italy, Julian Bailey and Kenny Acheson claimed seventh in the 90CK. Run by their European operation, NME, this would be the mainstay of Nissan's summer. But it wasn't enough. Despite a winter which had seen a new engine, the coming of top-notch recruits (and the going of Keith Greene) plus mega-money being spent trying to hoist the team to the top, there still seemed to be something fundamental missing; competitive finishes.

Toyota would have considered themselves lucky to have gotten away so lightly. After their favourite adopted son Geoff Lees notched his second successive Suzuka WSPC pole position it was all downhill from there. For sure, he managed fourth place on homeground sharing with reigning Japanese F3000 champion Hitoshi Ogawa but Toyota wanted, expected, more. But when they went to Monza all they got was a hefty repair bill, three chassies being written off, one by Geoff, two by Johnny Dumfries, in one of the biggest series of misfortunes ever to hit any team since Frank Spencer took up the sport.

Last year there were three Japanese makes slogging it out as much versus each other as against the infidel opposition. This year there were only two. Mazda were missing, upset by the FISA

Mercedes were out of luck at Silverstone despite leading handsomely early on.

edict which will see their efforts with rotary engines outlawed from the forthcoming new era and therefore electing not to contest the whole series. Taking an educated guess that Le Mans would go ahead out of the championship, which it ultimately did, they were not interested in supporting a series which did not support them.

Coming on top of the demise of the Proteus/Aston Martin team, it was the kind of snub no self respecting sanctioning body should dismiss lightly.

The born again Astons had returned to sports car racing less than a year earlier, their arrival initially tentative but gaining momentum as the season wore on, finally overtaking Jaguar as Top Brits. Now they were out, closed down, kaput. This despite the fact that a pair of AMR2s with their slightly modified tubs and heavily revised aerodynamics were already sitting on their Milton Keynes factory floor ready for action.

All manner of reasons were given for the demise, the on-off nature of Le Mans prominent amongst them. Other stories doing the rounds included Ford not wanting Aston to compete directly with Jaguar, both companies now controlled by Detroit. Another said that the team had been turned down for a Ford financed and Aston badged 3.5 litre engine they needed for the next generation of the WSPC. There were also comments made including about

being seriously over-budget. The real answer is, as is often the case in corporate politics, still clouded in mystery and will undoubtedly emerge in due course, possibly being a mixture of all these scenarios, perhaps more.

Most of the sixty plus staff managed to get jobs elsewhere, subsequently joining the NPTI attempt on Le Mans of Nissan USA. As a result, all the experience they had gained over the years would be put to good effect. But it would not be the same.

In two years time nor would sports car racing, the 3.5 litre 'Formula One' era due to begin in 1992, its start having been delayed a further season so as to give potential participants more time to ready themselves for the big time. Meanwhile, only Spice have seen fit to develop a challenger for the interim, their lightweight/unlimited fuel projectiles having impressed everybody last season without getting much by way of results.

Nothing seemed to have changed at Suzuka on that score either but at Monza a terrific performance by Wayne Taylor and new boy Eric van der Poele netted an excellent sixth, the team's second car probably showing equally as well if it had not been delayed after an altercation with a Toyota.

With FISA doing away with C2 there was no choice for the stalwarts of that category but to either move up or move out. Unfortunately for the likes of GPM

and Chamberlain who chose to do the former their full blown entree into the big league was not without its fraughter moments, neither having anything by way of positive results to show after the first two races. Nor would the results of the upcoming Silverstone or Spa encounters improve things by much. Undeterred, they would be at Le Mans and ready to do battle with all-comers.

Nor did any of their former C2 compadres do any better, the Alba with its Suburu F12 not able to qualify for any of the four pre-Le Mans WSPC races, the Spice of Berkeley, nee Kaleo, at least getting in but not much further than that. Neither would be seen at La Sarthe. As for ALD, they were simply themselves. If enthusiasm in the face of adversity won races the little French team would be consistent winners. As it is, they battle on bravely, usually getting nothing more rewarding than a whole host of problems to add to those they already have. Silverstone and Spa would be no different for them.

When the sports car circus arrived at the Northants track everyone knew that the status quo might be changing, although certainly not yet changed. Jaguar and the F1 Spices were getting closer to Mercedes, the World Champions for their part looking for their tenth straight win. It was not to be.

The second Mercedes did not even get to start. Both car #2 and driver Otto Schumacher (replacing Wendlinger)

were excluded for outside assistance from Sauber mechanics after stopping on the Copse Corner apron with gearchange difficulties during Saturday morning practice. Schumacher was also in trouble for failing to refasten his seatbelts before slowly driving around the track back to the pits for more permanent repairs. It was a harsh penalty to pay, one which mainly served to deprive the paying public of the opportunity to see a perfectly healthy race car. A deduction of points would have been far more appropriate.

One down, one to go. And go it did, Schlesser and Baldi totally unphased by the loss of their colleagues and leading handsomely until Mauro pulled off when the engine broke soon after taking over from Jean-Louis. C'est la vie.

This left Jaguar in the lead and although some would say it was a fortuitous win then they must remember the adage whereby to finish first then first you must finish. TWR had kept the pressure up and the Mercedes had cracked, a part of the valve gear to be precise. Brundle and Ferte brought the XJR11 home for its first victory one lap clear of Lammers and a particularly inspired Wallace. Their fourth straight WSPC win at their home venue, Jaguar's renaissance was all but complete.

Bruno Giacomelli and Fermin Velez netted third for Spice whose Tim Harvey/Wayne Taylor car again looked equally well poised until let down by a late engine failure. They would get some sort of consolation with an excellent fourth in Belgium a fortnight later. Spice, like Jaguar, were on the way up.

Nissan looked good for a top placing only for both cars to fall by the wayside in the last few laps, one with suspension failure, the other out of fuel. Although Mark Blundell managed to coax his arid beastie home on the starter motor its last lap was too slow to count and the car unclassified. People were beginning to get worried about those boys. All that money; all that effort; for what? Nothing much so far.

Joest took fourth, Wollek and Jelinski the sole survivors of the three 'works' cars which started out, Bernd Schneider and Steven Andskar fifth for Kremer, the final point going to Larrauri and Huysman. Brun's other two came home seventh and eighth. Nobody else had much to write home about.

Any postcard from Spa-Francorchamps would have read something to the effect that Mercedes had gotten their revenge but had been hard pressed by Martin Brundle who was only denied a probable victory by an engine bay fire, having led a lot of the early going. The win finally went to Mass and Wendlinger, the other Mercedes again suffering from an engine failure which dropped it to eighth. Lammers and Wallace took second for TWR.

Bailey and Acheson were a good third for Nissan. Although all the team were keen to stress that the four races thus far were only extensive testing programmes for Le Mans, there was a huge sense of relief that they had finally gotten a competitive finish at long last. Nissan had all but bought Le Mans and to fail ignominiously would be tantamount to total humiliation. And that would not do. At least now they could go off with some hope of getting the victory they prized above all others.

Yet if Nissan were concerned then Toyota must have been paranoid. Silverstone had been another calamity and Spa proved worse, Aguri Suzuki joining the company's unofficial metal benders and car crunchers club by adding another very damaged car to the three Monza wrecks. Often over on their fuel too, if ever a team had lost its way it must be Toyota.

Porsche duly filled out the bulk of the remaining places at the Coupes de Spa, Brun fifth, Lloyd sixth, Joest seventh and Kremer ninth behind the delayed Mercedes. The second Nissan took tenth. Despite numerical superiority the fact of the matter was that all of Porsche's efforts could not total more than fourteen points while Mercedes had twenty-seven, Jaguar nineteen. Yet whereas for Nissan and Toyota, and Spice for that matter, most saw their

'league' form as indicative of their 'cup' prowess, history has long since proven that the same train of thought cannot be levied against the Weissach Wonders.

When it comes to Le Mans, Porsche are different. Everyone knows that. They may have their backs against the wall in the silly little sprints, all four races so far this season not exceeding an aggregate of ten hours, but when it came to Le Marathon their record speaks for itself. Theirs would be a very hard act to follow and while the others may be quicker everyone knew that to win at La Sarthe first you had to defeat Porsche.

Mercedes would not because they were not going, the 1989 winners keeping to their word not to enter any non-championship race however important it might be. The cynics suggested that having scored an unexpected victory last time they were not willing to chance their luck again.

To say that their staying away would undermine someone else's victory was rubbish. They chose not to go. Bentley choose not to go, as do Ferrari, Alfa Romeo and many other great names from the past. The choice is theirs. As with life itself, you have to be in it to win it.

Jaguar were in it and determined to win it. Having lost out last year they were determined to rectify matters this time around, that splendid Daytona victory and the WSPC revival buoying their efforts. They knew it would not be easy, it never is. Porsche, for sure, were the biggest threat but over the course and over the distance Nissan or Toyota could rise to the occasion and do it, as could Mazda. There was nothing to be complacent about.

As the ferries and the hovercraft filled, all across Britain, all across the world, many questions were being asked about the week ahead. One was paramount : could Jaguar win Le Mans?

Jaguar's WSPC turbo car finally came good on home ground; an excellent fillip for Le Mans.

3.5 litres of turbocharged Jaguar V6 in all its glory.

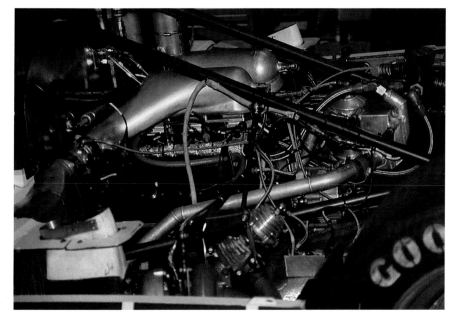

CRY FREEDOM

The person you had to feel sorry for was Nikolaus Durchworfen. Forty-five years old, a carpenter living in Volkerbund, East Germany, with his wife and two children, Niko was about to be denied the dream he nurtured almost as much as freedom itself.

For as long as he could remember one ambition had burned within his breast: to visit the Le Mans 24 Hours. Unfortunately, with the opportunities for travel beyond the barbed wired borders of his country *verboten* by the despotic regime under which he lived, even when Mercedes roared to victory for the Fatherland last June such an prospect seemed as far away as ever.

But if, as was once remarked, a week is a long time in politics, then six months is like an aeon. Between the success of the Silver Arrows and the turn of the year much had happened, not least of which being how that infamous symbol of oppression, the Berlin Wall, had come tumbling down, thereby opening up totally new and previous denied horizons to the millions of the Communist Bloc.

Throughout almost the whole of Eastern Europe, from the Deutsche Demokratisch Republik and Poland in the north by way of Czechoslovakia and Hungary to Rumania and Bulgaria in the south, ruthless dictators such as the Ceausescus and Erich Honicker had been cast aside, whole doctrinaire regimes eradicated. Albeit somewhat belatedly, once proud nations which had been suppressed by the fear of a late night knock on the door had woken to a new dawn and joined the twentieth century.

Now all that stood between Nikolaus and those of his ilk whose initiation to the joys of their new found liberty included nothing more bourgeois than a visit to a motor race, all that stood between him, between them, and their quest was one man. His name was Jean-Marie Balestre.

M.le President of FISA, the sport's governing body, a couple of years ago Balestre and his cohorts had belatedly realised that there was more to motor sport than mere Grands Prix. FISA started to take an interest in sports cars.

Much of what had been done since then has been good for the category, notably that teams be required to contest the whole series, not only those races they deemed fit to honour with their presence. Race organisers could now promote forthcoming events with a high degree of certainty regarding the entry, a much more palatable proposition than the 'will they or won't they' of previous years.

Less acceptable was the fact that a lot of the promised drum beating did not happen. You could stand in Northampton High Street on the day of the Silverstone WSPC race and not know it was going on. At the likes of Spa and Jarama you could probably stand outside the circuit yet still have no inkling.

Not so the ACO. Amongst the demands made on race organisers was the giving up of television and other commercial activities to FISA. The ACO said 'non'. They knew, as did everyone else, that their race, the Le Mans 24 Hours, was worth more than all the other World Sports Prototype Championship rounds put together, and they were keeping what they'd got, thank you very much.

After much quarrelling Le Mans was struck from the 1989 WSPC. On the face of it FISA had lost. They were determined it would not happen again. This time the battling started early, last year's race hardly over before the first salvoes were fired.

Back and forth went the letters, to and fro came the press releases, the mania of the situation reflected in the way that when they wanted to EMPHASISE certain POINTS each side did so by PUTTING them in CAPITAL letters. Then, around Christmas, as the world rejoiced over the fall of the Marxist tyranny, Balestre announced that he had been insulted by a follower of the ACO camp and without a full apology there would be no race, whatever the outcome of the negotiations.

Sacre Bleu! Previously intrenched empires were tumbling down around our ears but all that concerned M. Balestre was his honour. Until then he would hold the sport to ransom. Added to his on-going battle with F.1. ace Ayrton Senna which had degenerated to a similar low level, fortunately for the tattered dignity of global motor sport the world at large chose in the main to ignore him.

But motor sport could not, much as though it might want to. In what appeared to be an effort to deflect criticism from his stance over the supposed insult as anything else, suddenly it was announced that there was no way the ACO were going to hold any race with the circuit the way it was. A new FISA regulation plucked out of thin air declared that no straight could exceed two kilometres, thereby scuppering the famous Mulsanne which was over six. Safety was used as the excuse, as if FISA needed one. The ACO would need to install two chicanes by April if they were to stand any hope of getting a track licence. When they reluctantly but firmly agreed to do just that, Balestre went back to his insistence on getting an apology too.

Local politicians got involved, national politicians got involved, the pride of France was at stake. There was talk of using the silly little Bugatti Circuit, protests on the streets of Le Mans.

When everyone assembled in America for the Daytona 24 the mood amongst the press and participants was one of shock and horror. Even when the IndyCar teams were fighting with the USAC back in the late seventies, a battle which eventually saw the formation of the breakaway CART which now runs the World Series, *NEVER EVER* was there any thought or threat that the Indianapolis 500 would not take place. When it came right down to the nitty-gritty everyone knew what the bottom line was.

In the end the whole thing blew over. None except those present at the very highest levels – who included Roger Bambuck, the French Minister of Sport – will ever know what really went on behind those closed doors in the corridors of power. It is reliably suggested that more than a few skeletons were rattled in more than one cupboard before all parties eventually came to their senses and a compromise was reached.

Everyone got basically what they wanted. The ACO got their 24 Hours, FISA showed their muscle in good time for the next round of talks which would undoubtably start immediately after this year's event was over. The teams got the jewel in the sponsorship crown and the public their highlight of the year.

As for Balestre's apology, amongst the inevitable tirade of press releases and statements was one disassociating the club from the comments made by one of their allies. It somehow put the lid on the whole sorry affair.

As for Nikolaus Durchworfen, he got to go to the most famous motor race in the world. But it was a very close run thing.

And everyone lived happily ever after. Until the next time. . . .

CITY LIMITS

There is more to Le Mans than it being the place where they run the world's most famous race.

Situated on the confluence of the Sarthe and the Huisne rivers some 120 miles south-west of Paris, Le Mans and its environs is home for 150,000 people, a substantial number of whom work at a major car manufacturing plant set up by Renault in 1936. Known also as an important centre of the insurance industry, the city is also a major arts and cultural centre. Cosmopolitan, yet still unmistakably French, it has a long and colourful history.

Centred on a ridge overlooking the waters, there is evidence that people lived thereabouts back in the dawn of civilisation, the area subsequently being fortified by the Romans in the 2nd Century A.D. Originally known as Vindinum, then Subdunum, soon the wooden defences were replaced by a stone wall, complete with posterns and buttress towers, much of which still exists today. It would not be until the 12thC, after a number of other name changes including to that of Cenomanis in recognition of some of the earliest inhabitants of the area, that the town would become known as Le Mans.

Up to sixty-five feet high with a base over twelve feet thick, the sandstone/limestone decorated walls enclose an area of about twenty-five acres. An important staging post of the early merchant routes, the fortifications would serve generations of inhabitants well over the ensuing centuries as they fought off attacks from marauding Franks and Vikings.

Not that everyone came to plunder and pillage, St.Julian arriving about sixteen hundred years ago and bringing with him the first vestiges of Christianity, the bishops of his Abbeye du Pre amongst the foremost to organise the economic structure of the area. It is after St.Julian that the mighty Gothic cathedral which dominates the Place des Jacobins (the site of a former convent in which scrutineering has been held these past years) is named. Started in the 11thC and taking over four hundred years to complete, with its magnificent stained glass windows and two-tier Y-shaped flying buttresses the cathedral is rated amongst the best examples of its genre in all Europe.

British connections with the area are many, dating mainly from the period of William the Conqueror. Born in nearby Falaise, as the Duke Of Normandy he won the Battle of Hastings in 1066, thereby ascending to the throne of England. Some years later his grand daughter, Mathilda, the daughter of Henry I, married Geoffrey Plantagenent, Count of Anjou, the dowry including both Normandy and Maine, Le Mans then being the capital of the latter region.

The son of Geoffrey and Matilda was Henry Plantagenent. Born at Le Mans in 1133, he ascended to the throne of England as Henry II in 1154, reigning for thirty-five years. Although he did much to benefit both the Crown and its subjects, alas, history notes his most famous act as proposing the murder of Thomas a' Becket at Canterbury Cathedral. Mortified by the horror of what he had done, Henry then attempted to atone himself of the sin by building a number of charitable edifices, the splendid Hotel Dieu du Coeffort at Le Mans amongst them. Situated just off the Rue Nationale one kilometre south of St.Juliens, although now a church it was founded as a hospital-cum-poor-house for the town.

Married to Eleanor of Acquitaine (the former wife of King Louis VII of France) the pair had seven children including two very famous sons, Richard I – Richard the Lionheart – and John Lackland. No wallflower she, Eleanor was very politically aware and plotted with them against their father on matters she disagreed with her husband over, eventually being imprisoned for her actions.

For much of his life, including a substantial amount of his ten years reign, Richard was out of England fighting wars, most notably the Crusades, returning only to replenish his army and the fighting coffers. Indeed, his wife Berengaria, daughter of the King of Navarre, never ever set foot on English soil. After his death in 1199 while besieging the Castle of Chaluz, she retired from public life and eventually founded the Abbaye de l'Epau, some two miles east of Le Mans city centre.

John, an absolute tyrant of a man, who had tried to usurp the throne during Richard's absenses finally got the crown on the death of his brother and reigned until 1216, one year after being forced to sign the Magna Carta. It is John who, aided by his unsavoury cohort the Sheriff of Nottingham, is the villain of all the Robin Hood movies.

By now the town had outgrown its walls and was prospering and as such became an important strategic site, staying in the possession of the English kings right up until 1447. If the status quo had not changed, rather than be what is now referred to as 'A British Motor Race Held In France' the Vingt-Quatre Heures du Mans would be a British motor race held in Britain!

Throughout the Middle Ages (when it became a noted centre of cloth making, especially the dour black garb of clerics and lawyers gowns) one conflict then another visited Le Mans, the castle being destroyed on the orders of Louis XII in 1617. After that, things quietened down for a while only for the full horror of the French Revolution to reveal itself in December of 1793 when a royalist fighting force was cornered in the town, exhausted and hungry, by the republican army. In a night of slaughter thousands were killed, the now quiet and tourist filled streets of the beautifully restored old town within the city walls, Le Vieux Mans, running red with blood as Frenchman fought Frenchman on the streets of La Belle France.

More recently, the city withstood over four years of Nazi occupation before being liberated in August '44.

Although much of the history of the city is forever entwined with battles won and lost, a walk around Le Vieux Mans soon dispels any feelings of turmoil, the narrow cobbled streets with their abundance of well preserved 15thC Renaissance buildings a place of solitude and tranquillity far removed from the hustle and bustle of the modern city immediately beyond the Gallo-Roman walls. Half timbered houses, many now restaurants or boutiques, form an ideal counterbalance to the world outside, the more modern structures as typified by the town hall, Le Hotel de Ville, built in 1760 for the Counts of Maine

Not that all of Le Mans' claims on history are so ancient, local businessman Amedee Bollee and his son Amedee junior amongst the first pioneers of the motor car.

A place of contrasts, the opulent splendour of the interior of Le Palais des Congres et de la Culture in sharp contradiction to the austerity of the ancient benedictine abbey of Notre Dame de la Couture, the ultra modern and high-tech Mediatheque separated by half a mile and five hundred years from La Maison de la Reine Berengere, the city of Le Mans offers a lot to visitors with the time and inclination to explore it.

Almost enough to make you forget there's a motor race on!

STREET FIGHTING MEN

The people at the far end of the pitlane were looking distinctly worried.

The first of Thursday's two qualifying sessions was half over and their world had just been turned up side down on them. Thanks to the Repsol Brun Porsche 962.

Two years ago all the Le Mans tickets, posters and programmes had been adorned with a Silk Cut XJR9. Jaguar won the race. Twelve months ago the chosen marque had been Mercedes who then went on to record a historic victory. Buoyed probably as much by superstition and coincidence as anything else, Nissan were taking no chances and had bankrolled this year's event, hoping above hope that it would guarantee third time lucky.

Indeed, to emphasise their commitment they had arrived with no less than five 'works' cars (plus a pair of older versions to be campaigned by privateers) yet despite having the latest in whizz-bang up-to-the-minute technology it looked for all the world as if they might be upstaged by a design which should by now be more at home in a museum than heading the time sheets of the most famous motor race in the world. In the very first show of strength for the weekend ahead, that to claim the coveted pole position, their hopes had taken a sudden nose dive. Thanks to Oscar Larrauri.

There's no doubt about it, 'Popi' is a star. Dark and moody in the best South American tradition, the man from Sante Fe in the very heartland of Argentina may not have performed any miracles aboard the recalcitrant F.1. EuroBrun back in '88 but in one of 'Walti's' Porsches and he is transformed. Put him in with a shot at pole position and he will give it his all, however ancient the design of car he is driving, however unfashionable the team might have become. He may be harder on the cars than many, but then he is trying harder than most. He might not be the easiest guy to pass, but then he is there to lead, not follow. Once a racer, always a racer, that's Oscar Larrauri.

Aided by a special Andial prepared 3.2 litre turbo flat-six and a high downforce/short tail set-up, he wound up the Brun 962 to record a stunning 3m33.06s, chicanes and all, to take provisional pole position away from Geoff Brabham, the USA domiciled Aussie with the English accent having given Nissan the overnight honours with his Wednesday time of 3m33.28s.

Less than a quarter of a second yet it represented all the difference between delight and disaster as far as Nissan were concerned. With time running out they knew their chances of regaining the top slot were rapidly diminishing. But they wanted pole and were determined not to be denied, not even by 'Popi'. There was nothing left to do but play their ace. Enter Mark Blundell.

The great glowing ball of the sun was slowly sinking behind the tree line, the warmth of the day now giving way to the cool of the night, as he headed out onto the track in his specially prepared charger. It was 21H32 precisely.

Armed with a shade under one thousand horsepower of highly potent Nissan V8, more according to some, Blundell was determined to put the matter beyond all doubt. The youngest of all the Nissan drivers, 24 years old last April, and its most inexperienced campaigner too, having only transferred from motocross to Formula Ford six years ago, it was quite an accolade to be 'the chosen one'. Never before had he or Nissan, or any Japanese car for that matter, sat on the pole position of The Great Race. For the sake of himself, his team and all Japan he had to get it right. It was an awesome responsibility.

The great glowing ball of the sun was slowly sinking behind the tree line . . .

Off he went in a streak of red white and blur, taking every corner just right, every straight at maximum, only the briefest lift-off and down-change necessary when he came across a slow moving Cougar in the Porsche Curves seconds before flashing past the pits in a crescendo of speed and light. As he eased the pace and went onto his slow down lap up came the time on his cockpit computer readout: 3m27.02s – SIX seconds faster than anyone else! As far as qualifying went it was not so much a first pole as the last post.

Nissan had come, Nissan had seen and Nissan had conquered. Nobody, but nobody, was going to better that. Not even Larrauri. Indeed, without 'Popi' they would have had a clean sweep of the top two rows.

Joining the elated Blundell in the pole car was Julian Bailey, another young Englishman who for better or worse will take a long time to live down what most regard as a major indiscretion while trying too hard too early in the 1989 race. With them would be Gianfranco Brancatelli, the Italian moving over from Mercedes with whom he had taken second place last year.

Partnering 'Branca' on that weekend of so-near-yet-so-far had been Kenny Acheson. Unceremoniously dumped at the end of the season to enable Mercedes to pursue their 'Deutsche Kindchen' programme, the popular Irishman had soon found a home for himself with Nissan and on this occasion brought the #25 car into fifth on the grid despite having all manner of practice woes, notably transmission. Teamed with F.1. men Martin Donnelly and Oliver Grouillard, theirs would progress to watch if they could cure the problems and go the distance. If.

Both those cars were being run by Nissan Motorsports Europe, based in Milton Keynes, under the guidance of Dave Price. It was he who had played such a vital part in the success of Sauber Mercedes last year and was another of those lured by the yen into trying to repeat the exercise for Japan. Time would tell if he could.

Sandwiched between the two NME R90CKs were one each for Nissan Motorsports International – the Japanese driven one – and the first of the NPTI cars being run by the IMSA champions led by Don Devendorf. Every one of the three pronged attack, the British, the Japanese and the American teams, had been allowed their own development programme in the hope of producing a winner from amongst them and despite coming up with quite different solutions – notably the Japanese aerodynamics – all appeared to have come to very similar results. So far.

Masahiro Hasemi tried all he could to push the Brun 962 off the front row, failing by a mere 11/100ths of a second. Although it was not enough to achieve that, it was sufficient to demote Geoff Brabham and his co-drivers Chip Robinson and Derek Daly to fourth, the IMSA men preferring not to attempt to improve their time on the second day and electing to concentrate on their race set-up instead. Driven by three very experienced pilots and run by the double IMSA championship winning team (which included the last two

Sebring 12 Hours amongst their laurels) aided and abetted by Ray Mallock and many members of his Ecosse/Proteus operations, of all the Nissan entries this was the one the others feared most.

The other 'American' car, the #84 example for Michael Roe, Bob Earl and Steve Millen fared less well, gearbox problems restricting it to a lowly twenty-fifth. However, despite the relative inexperience of these three hereabouts (only Roe had seen the place before, last year with the Astons) there was no doubting that they could feature well given a clean run. Alas, it would not be but they would go home with more than they had bargained for.

So did Jonathan Palmer but of the type he would prefer to have done without. Early in Wednesday's first session the McLaren test driver had been on 'a flyer' down Mulsanne when at about 215 miles an hour it became one, the car in control of his destiny rather than the other way around. Hitting the barriers on both sides of the track JP's subsequent tales of hurtling through the branches of the overhanging trees bear testimony to a terrifying flight of over one hundred yards, the wreckage coming to a stop nearly a quarter of a mile from where the car had first got into difficulties.

Nursing a twisted ankle and a thumb broken by steering wheel whiplash, Palmer had been very lucky indeed. Not so the Porsche, one brand new car written off with less than an hour of running time logged against it. A rear suspension breakage was suspected.

The repurcussions were manyfold, not least of which was the transferring of co-drivers Bob Wollek and Philippe Alliot to other cars. As a result the much underrated Will Hoy once again missed out on the main chance, having to forfeit his seat in Joest #9 to 'Brilliant Bob'. One day 'Lady Luck' will choose to bestow her favours on the perenially unfortunate Hoy. There again, one day the sun will rise in the west. . . .

More serious regarding the overall tenor of the race, however, was the fact that Palmer's wreck had on the official 'works' Porsche team. After all, if the educated guess of a suspension breakage

The Repsol 962 started its week by blowing an engine on the very first lap of practice. Its race would end in a similar fashion.

was correct then this was not the first such problem of that type they had encountered, probably the third since March. To paraphrase Noel Coward, once is an incident, twice is an accident, three times is a downright disaster!

Immediately the other three Joest 962s were grounded to be checked over, the Absteinach team taking no chances. As a result they were unable to go through their complete programme of pre-race tests and not mount the challenge for pole position which had been expected of them. Returning to the fray some time later, Hans Stuck managed to nett third fastest by the end of the first day but with no improvement on Thurday this left him, Derek Bell and Frank Jelinski down in sixth on the final grid. It should have been better. It could have been worse.

Of the other two remaining Joest Porsches, neither really figured at all. The oldest crew in the race, their combined ages totalling 139 years, it was left to the elder statesmen Henri Pescarolo (here for his twenty-fourth start) and 'Jolly' Jacques Laffite to undertake most of the qualifying effort while their young-by-comparison renta driver Jean-Louis Ricci picked up the bills. They would start thirtieth.

Twelve places higher up, Wollek got the best he could out of the dark blue Mizuno car he was now to share with former winners Stanley Dickens and the pseudonymous 'John Winter' but it was not enough, eighteenth poor reward for a lot of effort. Hoping that some of their previous good fortune would rub of on him at this his twentieth attempt, Ivan Lendl might deserve to win Wimbledon, Bob Wollek definitely deserves to win Le Mans.

Not that Joest were making things easy for themselves or the 'Uncrowned King of Strasbourg', already the signs being that they had guessed wrong. They had come with their familiar low downforce *langheck* tails and been blown into the weeds by those of their own customers operating with the alternative high downforce/short tail arrangements, notably Brun.

Lining up alongside the 'Wollek' 962 on Row 9 was the last of the Jaguars. While the Nissans and the Porsches had been trying to fight over the top of the grid TWR had been getting on with their own business. Just like at Daytona. Not for them the frantic attempts to out-psyche and out-boost each other, their V12 engined XJR12LMs primed not for the fleeting glory of a few minutes but the everlasting kudos of twenty-four hours.

Earlier in the week the team had caused quite a stir when they unloaded a turbo car but there was never any real consideration given to running any XJR11s here. It was one of three they had brought with them en route to Jarama where the WSPC were due to race the following weekend. When, late on Thursday, that event was cancelled the news was greeted with the same mixed emotions by TWR personnel as everybody else in pitlane. They were pleased at not having to face the prospect of another race so soon after the 24 Hours, itself only a fortnight on from Spa, but annoyed at the timing and tenor of the cancellation.

A lot of teams had spent a lot of time and money preparing for the non-existant event, ferries and hotels already booked and prepaid. No reasons were given for the cancellation, only excuses. FISA said the track was unfit, but it had been perfectly alright when Brun tested there only a few weeks ago. Another story doing the rounds was that the sponsor had pulled out due to the race date clashing with Spain's participation in the World Cup. That had been known *MONTHS* before.

Many people simply reckoned that in the ongoing war versus the ACO the race had been put on at its most inconvenient date to (hopefully) cause the maximum disruption to the Le Mans entry and when it failed to dissuade most teams from going to France the same bloody-mindedness had cancelled the event. True or not, it is a terrible indictment on the way the sport is run that this is what so many people believed. . . .

GEOFF BRABHAM (NISSAN #83) : "We looked to have pole position for a while but for the second day decided we were just going to work on our race set-up and fuel mileage, etcetera. We are happy where we are starting, fourth, which is pretty good considering we do not know too much about the car, this being our first attempt with it. I think we are going to be competitive and have a strong race.

"As for changing from car to car, our new IMSA car (the NPT90) is running very well, straight out of the box. We won the last race with it (at Mid-Ohio) which was only the third one it went into so we are happy with that. The old car, I know like a glove. This one, the Group C one, has a lot less downforce and as we don't have the fuel restriction in IMSA or run on a track as fast as this the car does feel a lot different but it's no problem. As for preferences, the ground rules are the same for everybody and I prefer any race where I have a chance to win. I think we can win this one."

KAZUYOSHI HOSHINO (NISSAN #23) : "Tomorrow we attack!"

STEVE MILLEN (NISSAN #84) : "I love it, it's just a giant street race and I love street racing. It's a fantastic place. It's what I imagined it to be although slower in a lot of areas than what I had pictured. That surprised me, I imagined it to be more sustained high speed. The Nissan is a good and reliable car. We did not try and do a great qualifying effort on it and I am very proud to be here with them."

JAN LAMMERS (JAGUAR #2) : "In the race there will be cars which have less potential to run to the fuel and there will be less spread between the first, second and third drivers. They will also have different engines. So I am pretty convinced that our race effort will be very good."

ANDY WALLACE (JAGUAR #2) : "Everything has been perfect; no problems. We weren't interested in a qualifying position at all, it means absolutely nothing. The more you take out of your car in qualifying the more you take out of it for the race so that is why we are seventeenth.

"I have probably been very lucky with 24 Hours races. Our plan is to keep the car together, driving as fast as we can without destroying the car and that has seemed to have worked at the other 24 Hours races. If you abuse a car early on you will have problems so if anybody watching the race wonders why were are not leading the first lap the reason for that is simple, we want to be leading at the end."

Mark Blundell created some sort of record at Le Mans this year, becoming the youngest person ever to snatch pole position for the race. It was by most accounts also by the biggest margin of all time, over six seconds clear of the field. With over one thousand horsepower balanced on a knife edge, it was a superb performance by the Williams F.1. test driver.

"I had never tested a car with that amount of power before. We had quite a bit on Wednesday when we were doing three minutes thirty-threes but never that much. It was just banzai, first lap out and I did the time.

"I came out of the pitlane in fourth position. I would have liked to have come out first but soon got through the other cars which were in front of me and that gave me a clear lap. I got no traffic whatsoever until the Porsche Curves where I had to do a down change from fourth to third. It was a Cougar.

"The car was quite stable although it reacted quite badly over the bumps because of the power it had, so trying to lay the power down onto the track at bumpy parts of the circuit like the first chicane was quite a handful. I had a couple of opposite locks on during that lap. Apart from that it wasn't too bad!

"I did not realise it was *that* quick, expecting maybe a three minutes thirty or thirty-one. When the black box on the instrument panel came up twenty-seven I did not believe it so I radioed back to confirm. I was very pleased. Nissan were too.

"It'll look good in my c.v. !"

While some contemplated the prospect of an unexpected weekend off, there was still the not inconsiderable matter of getting through this event first. To many, TWR were starting as favourites, not so much due to their improved WSPC and IMSA form of late but that of the last five such 24 Hours events, both in Europe and America, Mercedes had won one, Porsche had won one, Jaguar had won three. There again, they had started both of last year's races as favourites but gone home with their tails between their legs.

Not that things got off to a particularly good start when John Nielsen lost a wheel at the Porsche Curves on Wednesday, fortunately without damaging himself or the car. Not for the first time either; it had happened at Daytona eighteen months before. Then he had gone on to finish second, now he was determined to put the matter behind him and come out on top. Partnered by his regular co-driver Price Cobb and also Eliseo Salazar, the Chilean being asked back again after acquitting himself well last year, this car was being run by the IMSA team from Indiana and as such differed in set-up from the other Kidlington run machinery by virtue of having alternative roll bars and suspension geometry. Lining up ninth on the two-by-two grid, the differences would serve Jaguar #3 well.

Immediately ahead, filling Row 4 were two more of the Silk Cats, Martin Brundle pipping 'Super John' by fractions in the Number #1 car he was to share with Alain Ferte and Jaguar newcomer David Leslie (the Scot a refugee from Ecosse and Aston Martin and as such having his first big league ride of the season) yet having to give best to Davy Jones aboard Jaguar #4 who recorded a fine 3m36.10s to lead the Silk Cut brigade.

The rapid young American was listed to share with Michel Ferte, Alain's older brother, and Luis Perez Sala. Unfortunately the former Minardi Grand Prix man (sixth at Silverstone last year) was unable to cut *la moutarde* and with his times way off the pace of the others was quietly sidelined from the equation.

There must be something of a love-hate relationship between TWR and Spain. Mainly the latter. Back in 1986, the infamous 'Derek Warwick Accident' at Jerez had ultimately proved to deny both driver and team of World Championship titles. At the same circuit two years later, Sauber Mercedes finally came of age and scored a superb victory over the Jags, one from which they have never looked back. Also in 1988, Fermin Velez destroyed a XJR9 while testing at Silverstone.

Only this week, the Jarama race had been cancelled and now the country's top driver had proven unable to make the grade at Le Mans. If you had sung 'Viva Espana' within earshot of anybody remotely connected to TWR just then you were in mortal danger of being invited to put your head between your knees and whistle up your Barcelona!

Although phasing out Sala relieved TWR of one burden, that of having to compensate for a slow driver, it obviously put extra strain on the others, the overwhelming consensus of opinion being that with its new chicanes Le Mans was now as arduous as Daytona and therefore in need of a three man team to share the work load. As a consequence, Tom Walkinshaw and his inner sanctum decided that at least for a couple of their charges they would leave the third driver in reserve thereby giving themselves the chance to switch men around should circumstances dictate late in the race. It was a shrewd move.

Although Spain and the Spaniards might not be flavour of the decade at Kidlington, there is no doubting that Dutchmen fair much better, especially Jan Lammers. Yet while the other three XJRs hogged the grid immediately behind the qualifying heroes from Nissan and Porsche, the little big man from Zandvoort was to be found down in seventeenth.

Allowed by an enlightened regime to plot their own strategy, Jan and his co-drivers Andy Wallace and newcomer Franz Konrad had elected to go at it *soto voce*. The thinking was that by putting the absolute minimum of strain on Jaguar #2 in practice it would be in better shape for the race so while they were a full three seconds adrift of their Silk Cut counterparts none of them were looking at all worried about it, the mood very relaxed and optimistic. Just like at Daytona.

Not that their practice sessions were without any exciting moments, Lammers falling in with John Nielsen on Wednesday evening and the pair of them to be seen sliding the rear ends in tandem like a pair of syncronised swimmers as they powered out of Mulsanne Corner together. 'Just having some fun' was how the Dutchman would later describe it, his Danish colleague smiling in unison at the memory.

On the grid next to the 'Nielsen' XJR was the top Toyota. Twelve months ago the Japanese team had tried for pole position only to suffer the indignity of having its time ruled out for using a T-car. This time they too decided to forgo the fleeting glories of qualifying to concentrate on their race set-up. The cynics suggested that there was no way they were likely to be able to match Nissan anyway so to have not taken up the challenge would mean less loss of face than if they had tried and failed. Such are the corporate machinations of motor racing, Japanese style.

Having been unable to get any of their three cars beyond Saturday night last time, actually it was a wise move. As a result, they came armed only with the 3.2 litre units instead of the bigger V8s they have on offer, Geoff Lees doing the best for the Toyo aboard its blue #36 Minolta machine.

Two rows further back F.1. man Aguri Suzuki set the grid time for the Taka-Q #37 car he was to share with former winner Johnny Dumfries and saloon ace Roberto Ravaglia while on the row beyond that the Keith Greene managed SARD entry owed its position to another former G.P. man, Pierre-Henri Raphanel doing the honours there.

In amongst all the Jaguars and Toyotas were a whole host of Porsches, the gorgeous looking Nisseki sponsored car of Trust Racing on Row6 alongside the Kenwood Kremer car qualified by Sarel van der Merwe. The other Kremer brothers entry, looking for all the world like an explosion in a paint factory, took up position seven places back, Philippe Alliot having transferred over from Joest after Palmer's dramas to head the crew of the Number #11 car. If it went as well as it looked he was in for a good ride.

Richard Lloyd's team were all at sevens and elevens according to their row placings, the piquant pink Italya #43 car of RLR stalwart James Weaver, 1989 winner Manuel Reuter and F.1. coming man JJ Lehto – who was having his first race of any type with a roof over

his head – making thirteenth. Meanwhile, John Watson and Bruno Giacomelli were joined in the team's #44 car by Allen Berg but none of them could better twenty-first.

With the former in high downforce/short tail trim and the later sporting the low downforce/high tail bodywork RLR seemed to be playing for a draw hoping to win a penalty shoot-out rather than going for goal. It is five years since the Silverstone team came second in The Great Race and with the growth of the 'works' teams Lloyd seem to have lost their way somewhat, the trick or treat of their two entirely different set-ups emphasising the point.

Obermaier were fifteenth and twenty-eighth, Essen taxi driver Harald Grohs setting an excellent time in the #26 car despite being first to visit the kitty litter at the new chicanes. His time was thanks to having an Andial qualifying engine as per Larrauri. The other Porsche in the top twenty was the Alpha 962, the team deciding to do the job themselves this year having been very disappointed with the result of last year's foray with Brun. Tiff Needell led the charge for the A-team, accompanied by David Sears and newcomer Anthony Reid. This time last year Reid was doing Vauxhall Lotus.

The middle of the grid was filled out by two Cougars and Nissan #82, all three running under the auspices of Yves Courage, while the other private Nissan – operated by the appropriately named Team Le Mans – faired slightly better in twenty-fourth courtesy of Takeo Wada. The ACO have taken to calling their race 'The World Event' and with Wada sharing with Anders Olofsson of Sweden and Maurizio Sandro Sala from Brazil, the TLM car had really taken the message to heart.

Four rows behind them came the 3.5litre/750 kgs Spice C1, the team knowing before they even set foot in the place that they were in for a hard time of it. Despite a fairly quiet practice neither Tim Harvey, Chris Hodgetts or Fermin Velez could break into the top thirty, lining up on Row16 alongside the second Schuppan 962, the Omron one. Vern's Takefuji #33 was not much higher in the overall scheme of things, 1977 and '83 Hurley Haywood winner making the grid time in a car he was to share with F3000 hot shot Rickard Rydell and Wayne Taylor, the latter fast making a big name for himself on the IMSA scene these days. Both the Schuppan cars broke engines in practice, hence their low positions, but could well have been looked on as dark horses

if things went well for them in the race. They didn't.

Nor do they ever seem to for the Lancia or Team Davey's pair of Porsches. Turbo problems; engine problems; gearbox problems; despite all the enthusiasm in the world the Italians were struggling just to make the grid, Magnani surviving a coming together with unyielding armco to secure a place on Row19. The way things would turn out, he might be forgiven for wondering if it was worth it.

As for Tim Lee-Davey, what can one say other than neither of his hastily prepared 962s were able to break the four minute barrier, the not-so-Supercad version making it into forty-first, the Marukatsu example only being allowed in as 'Tail End Charlie' at the discretion of the organisers after failing to make the 130% qualifying rule. Four years ago the ACO had been less accomodating to Tim's efforts with the troublesome Tiga Turbo but this time the obviously felt sorry for him.

CHIP ROBINSON (NISSAN #83) : "I was about 150m behind him (Palmer) and could see a car bouncing down the guardrail. There were tyres and bodywork flying everywhere and it was such a mess that the marshals just stopped everybody else from going by. We were doing about 200 mph down there so he was really lucky."

TIM HARVEY (SPICE #21) : "Our intention is to finish. We are not running Cosworth DFR Formula One engines but basically what are 3½ litre C2 engines. It is the only thing which has a chance of finishing 24 Hours. It is a data acquisition exercise for us."

J J LEHTO (PORSCHE #43) : "I have never done any Group C or saloon racing before, driving the car for the first time during Thursday qualifying. Its quite a bit different to single seaters, much heavier, you have to save the fuel and everything. It's cruising but it's fun."

MANUEL REUTER (PORSCHE #43) : "We had no special problems in qualifying. We are running the sprint version which I think is the right compromise for this race."

JOHNNY HERBERT (MAZDA #202) : "I have only done the night session so far so I don't know where I am going yet. I have to learn. the Mazda is good to drive compared to a Porsche which is like a tank. They are heavy and slow, the Mazda is a lot more 'darty' so it's pretty good. I am looking forward to it.

"Driving a Mazda is also a guarantee I'll do 24 Hours. We could do a forty-eight hour race and it would still carry on. . . ."

STEFAN JOHANSSON (MAZDA #201) : "It is quite an easy car to drive so it is not a problem settling in. I was surprised at the engine power it has."

JESUS PAREJA (PORSCHE #16) : "Everything is okay. We think we will have a good race."

ROGER SILMAN (JAGUAR TEAM) : "We could not have hoped for anything better and are looking forward to the race very much."

Mazda #202 lined up on Row11 thanks to Grand Prix men Bertrand Gachot, Johnny Herbert and Volker Weidler.

Lancia had a troubled practice. The race would be even more fraught for this much rebuilt machine.

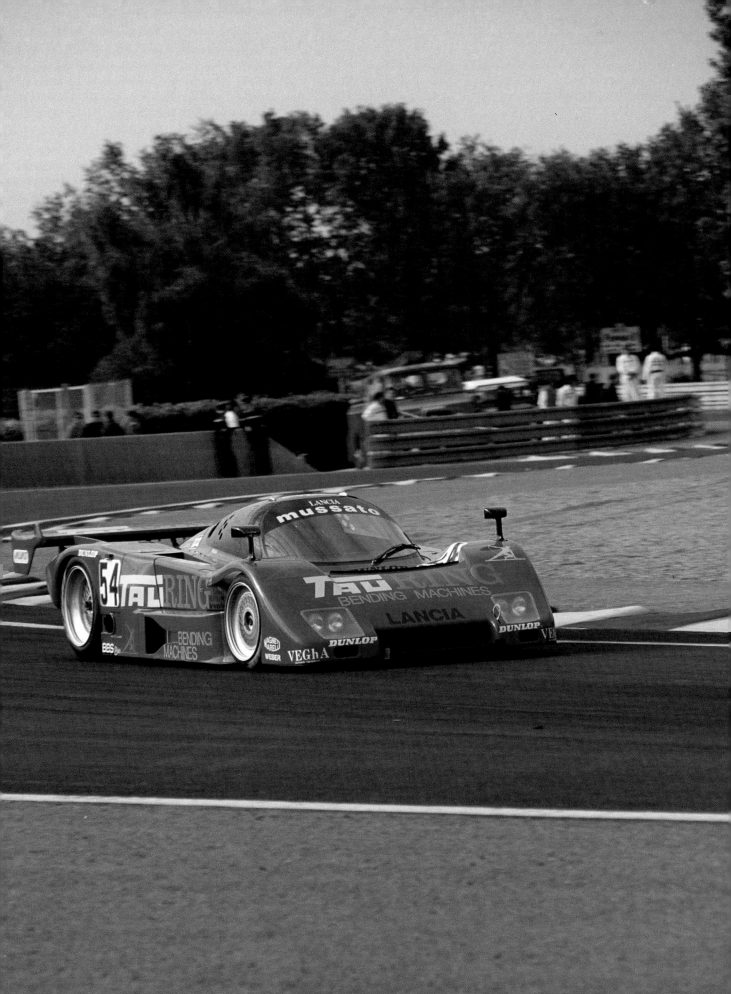

Max Cohen-Olivar brought some light relief to proceedings by adopting a samurai headband for the week while the question most being asked about Team Davey was regarding the size of the bag of gold Katsunori Iketani had handed over to secure his place after the devastation he had caused in his brief sojourn with the team at last year's event. The overwhelming conclusion was that it must have been very big indeed.

The IMSA category was, as expected, Mazda, Mazda, Mazda all the way, their drivers including F.1. names Bertrand Gachot, Johnny Herbert, Stefan Johansson and Volker Weidler alongside the more regular pilotes such as David Kennedy and Yojiro Terada. Based on their stunning performance twelve months ago many learned observers reckoned they might be reliable enough and quick enough for a place in the top five, possibly even better if circumstances and the weather played into their rice bowl. With an array of talent like theirs all things were possible, the six Eurostars taking the pair of stunning new superfast 787s while an all-Japanese crew relied on one of last year's 767Bs, albeit upgraded.

At least this time they would have some class opposition, the last few victories being only internal affairs. Ranged against Mazda was Momo, an IMSA spec–962 owned and raced by Gianpiero Moretti who was returning to La Sarthe for the first time since 1970. Helping him out was Gunther Gebhardt whose brother Fritz was in charge of the car's preparation, and Nick Adams, the London based loss adjuster having his first outing in a Porsche and conducting himself with aplomb (particularly during the night sessions) when allowed to play by the other two. After a very careful practice, they qualified thirty-fifth.

Actually, the most exciting part of Momo's week was not on the track but in the paddock. Late on Wednesday afternoon Moretti, the money man, had arrived and been mortified by what he saw. Fritz had done a deal with Raika and instead of the glorious red coachwork with yellow arrows the nose and sides were now hideous black. It looked terrible!

Luckily for those with delicate sensibilities the conversation which followed was mainly in German but the gist of it was clear to anyone without translation necessary. Too late to do anything that afternoon before practice began, suffice is to say that come the Thursday sessions Porsche #230 was back in its normal livery and looking superb. By way of a postscript, the Raika name, its dour black colour scheme and money would subsequently find its way onto the 'works' Spice C1 car for the race. The sum rejected by Moretti and taken up by Spice was whispered to be £50,000. . . .

Lining up alongside the Momo machine as top of C2 was Spice #103, John McNeil's Mako team firm favourites for class honours and a full seven seconds clear of Pierre-Alain Lombardi's similar car. Understandably happy with the way things went during qualifying, Mako would change from a 3.5 litre DFL to a 3.3 unit for the race. It would do them no favours.

Third in C2 was another French Spice, the Graff car, while three more British versions, namely those of Chamberlain, PC Automotive and GPM were all more than capable of a good result despite not showing particularly strongly during qualifying. The rest of the forty-nine car grid was filled with a variety of projectiles, Cougar and ALD trying to uphold local honour, ADA and Tiga fighting to keep the British flag flying high.

And a cow jumped over the moon.

GPM had also brought along a C1 Spice but both its engines lasted about as long as a snowflake in hell, much to the annoyance of Dave Prewitt and Roy Baker, and thereby joining the Palmer 962 amongst the non starters. Another not to make the grade was the 'works' Argo in which Ian Khan had started putting in some respectable lappery before handing over to the blonde bombshell, French hillclimber Anne Baverey who ignored the tacho redline of 9,500, the 'tell-tale' stuck at twelve-. This made team manager Gordon Horn very unhappy.

The only good thing to come out of it all was the increase in the lady's knowledge of the English language. Or was it her Anglo-Saxon? With the team's third driver below the cut-off point, they were forced to withdraw the car, moves to get former Argo exponent Will Hoy in the cockpit coming to nowt.

As did the Norma. It was supposed to be fitted with the MGN W12 engine of which there was no sign, the car not venturing beyond its paddock tent all week except for scrutineering. What it had in the back then is anybodys guess, much of the fun of the week being the unofficial game of 'Spot The W12'. Nobody ever did. For days on end every peek into their little world would reveal a chassis with wheels and a transmission with wheels, never the bit in between. Finally, the beleaguered little team issued a press release saying that the engine had not run due to electrical problems. And a cow jumped over the moon.

More disappointing was the loss of the Canary. Not bright yellow but plain white, Paul Canary's old Lola Corvette caused quite a sensation when it arrived at scrutineering, until then nobody believing it really existed. Unfortunately that was when its woes started, the car failing to get a 'pass' and having to be heavily modified especially with regards to the nose area and rollover structure, this work going on well into Wednesday afternoon. Indeed, even when the car appeared in the pitlane for practice later that same day it still did not have any official stickers on. Not that it mattered much in the end, only completing a handful of laps over the course of the two days, its best some ninety seconds off the back of the grid.

What the public had clamoured to see and hear was the engine. All ten-point-two litres of it! Designed ostensibly for drag racing, unfortunately the Eagle V8 was not upto the task, blowing two pistons on its first outing. This required a change to the 'smallblock' unit of a mere 9.4 litres but, alas, to no avail. Theirs had been an audacious attempt to rock the status quo and had failed on almost every count but Le Mans '90 was all the better for them having been there.

So it was over for another year, the grid finally sorted and fixed. As they made their final preparations for the weekend everyone speculated as to what it all meant, trying to find a winner from amongst all the signs so far.

The chances of Spice and Cougar springing a surprise were considered remote at best, those of Toyota and Mazda much better yet still unlikely. As for Nissan, the story went that following their impressive qualifying performances a telegram – or was it a fax? – had been received from Tokyo stating words to the effect of 'Well Done. Now We Expect You To Win The Race'. The only thing it did not say was 'Or Else'.

Part closed circuit, part open road, in the opening skirmishes of the 1990 Battle of Le Mans the 8½ mile Circuit de la Sarthe had already exacted a high toll from some, gone easy on others. The weekend would be different, for sure.

Some would rise to the occasion as others fell by the wayside, of that there was no doubt. Fought in automotive terms it would be a glorious contest between the men and machinery of the old world and the new. Would the rising of the sun on Saturday morning herald the dawn of a new era or would the old guard chez Porsche and Jaguar win through once again? Not even the soothsayers or shinto priests knew the answer to that one. Yet.

*Last year's C2 victor, the Cougar would
be out of luck this time.*

*Smoke gets in your eyes. GPM'S Spice
C1 consumed engines as if there was no
tomorrow. For it there wasn't. . . .*

PICTURE POST

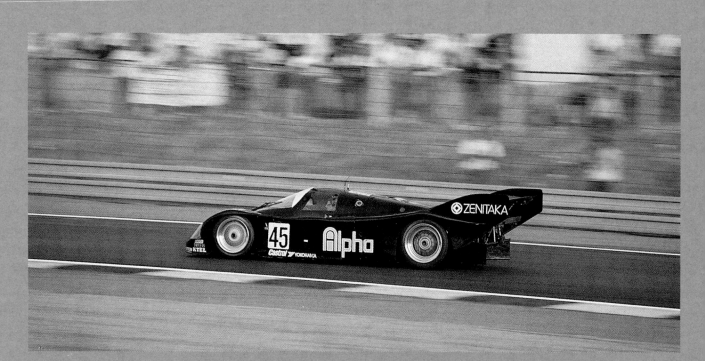

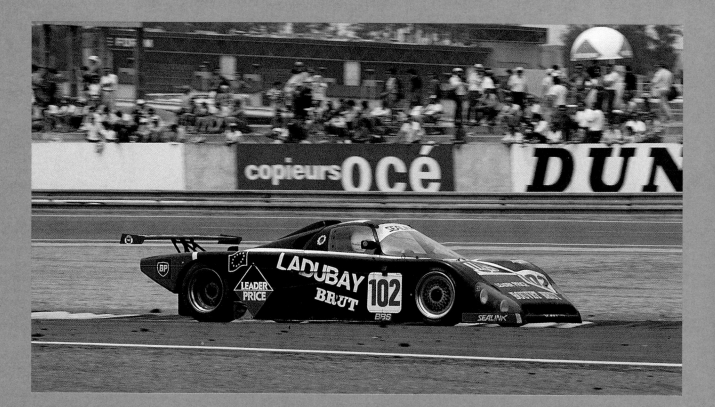

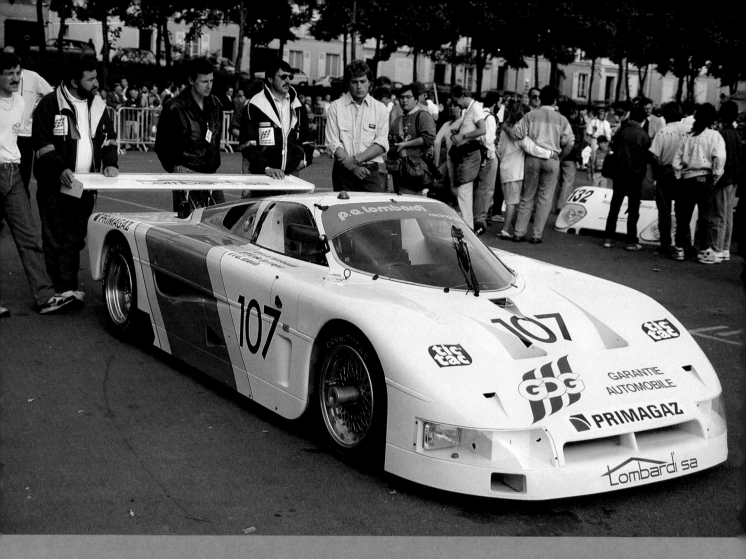

THE THIRD MAN

"No doubt I will be called upon to do the first double night stint. . . ."

Nick Adams was reflecting on what had been and contemplating what was to come. Although seated only a few yards up the Le Mans paddock from his normal abode chez Chamberlain, the reigning C2 World Champion was a long way from home. This time it would be different; he had accepted an offer to drive the Momo Porsche 962 in the IMSA GTP category against a trio of omnipotent Mazdas.

The run up to Le Mans is always something of a meat market with drivers trying to get the best and most competitive rides from teams, the teams trying to get the best and most competitive drivers. Sponsorship and money only add to the melee.

Hopefully the deals will be struck in sufficient time for them to do a test session or two together, perhaps even a race. With seemingly identical cars from the same stable often feeling like very different animals, the move to something totally alien to anything you had even sat in before let alone driven means that anyone who turns up at somewhere as arduous as Le Mans without such experience is having their work cut out for them. The best adapt, the others flounder, even a recent Grand Prix point scorer unable to make the grade in a Jaguar this time around, despite having previously tested in an XJR. The baptism of fire is harder than it might first appear to the layman and as the 1990 race drew closer, the name of Nick Adams was on a few shopping lists with good reason.

Three years ago, in 1987, he had recorded a scorching C2 pole position in Hugh's Spice Hart turbo, going even better twelve months later when putting a lot of top C1 runners to shame. Last year, partnered by Fermin Velez (his WSPC co-champion) and Gigi Taverna in a Cosworth V8 powered version, they had led the class by so much for so long only to be let down by engine failure when it seemed easier to win than to lose.

Having therefore made somewhat of a name for himself, the London based insurance loss adjuster had been sought out by three teams for their 1990 assaults on La Sarthe, a mixture of timing and circumstances finding him contracted to Momo Gebhardt Racing. The car was owned by the noted steering and road wheel manufacturer Gianpiero Moretti who would also be one of the three nominated drivers, the other being Gunther Gebhardt whose brother Fritz was in charge of its preparation. Nick had driven for the Gebhardts before, in their home built C2 machines in the mid-eighties, but this was big league.

"For me it is a good experience and I will use it to my best advantage" he commented at the beginning of the week. "I will be able to go to other teams and say I have raced at Le Mans in a Porsche 962." Such things count for a lot in the sports car pecking order, Franz Konrad said to have gotten the verdict over several others for the twelfth Jaguar seat by virtue of his Porsche experience, the Spice drivers rumoured to have been dismissed by TWR as lightweights.

It was the classic dilemma of the newly hired top gun . . .

Yet it is no laughing matter to contemplate driving a 200 miles an hour projectile that you hardly know. The first time Nick had ever sat in the car he was soon to be racing around the clock in all weathers was on Wednesday afternoon. Indeed, until then he admits to never ever having sat behind the steering wheel of any Porsche before, be it road or race!

Not that it got him very far, all the seat time in the first of Wednesday's two sessions being entirely dominated by Moretti and Gebhardt, 'NADAMS' standing around watching and waiting for the call which did not come. It was the classic dilemma of the newly hired top gun versus the entrenched old stagers.

Nick had plenty of experience thereabouts, this being his sixth consecutive attempt at the race. What is more, despite never yet having been classified as a finisher his cars had logged up an impressive seventy-two hours of race action between them before bowing to their various fates. New chicanes or not, He knew his way around Le Circuit de La Sarthe alright.

Moretti, however, had only visited the place once before, the 50-years old Milanese enthusiast having done the 1970 event aboard a private Ferrari 512S which succumbed to transmission problems in the night. Much had changed since then. As for Gunther Gebhardt, the former German Formula Super Vee champion had not even done that, being known more for the cars he and Fritz construct and prepare than any driving prowess. He was a Le Mans rookie.

Two drivers were very familiar with the car but not the track while the other knew the circuit but had never driven a 962 before. All needed seat time. No doubt a decisive factor was that the first two were the car owner and the co-principal of the team which ran it. There was nothing left for Nick to do than be patient and philosophical. He had been around the racing scene long enough to know the way it is.

"The purpose of the weekend as far as I am concerned – and I hope to hell I don't regret these words as I am tempting fate – is to turn in a steady and reliable peformance rather than anything dramatic. I'm sure that is what the team want out of me and that is what I am hoping to give them.

"The role of the third driver is always that the team believes he can do a competent job without having to be spoon fed along the way. You do your stints as required and it is assumed, because they have chosen you, that you can do it on the fuel and bring it back in one piece."

When they finally let him have a go during the darkness of the later session he did not bring it back at all. Only three laps into his familiarisation stint the clutch exploded stranding him out by the first Mulsanne chicane for the rest of the period. So not only did the third driver not get a fair go but Porsche #230 only occupied thirty-eighth place on the grid, a full eleven seconds down on the slowest Mazda, the other two so far ahead they could have been in the stratosphere.

Fortunately things improved on Thursday, changes to the rear wing and electronic management system microchip moving it along to a 3m49.96 (set by Gebhardt) and within reasonable striking distance of their foes in the IMSA GTP class war, the gap even to the best of them now only seven seconds. The Momo Porsche would line up in thirty-fifth position next to the top C2 car.

"For the first time I had a series of laps and really got into it, after which I was much happier. It really handles well. Once I had done about five laps I was totally at home with it, everything fitting into place."

So much so that in Thursday's late session he set the quickest night time for the car, easily outpacing his two team mates despite still being very aware of the edict to 'bring it back in one piece'. It was a job well done.

"You have to have self belief to do this job but there is nothing like having done it to satisfy yourself that it's not going to be a problem."

Not that he thought it would be so straight forward when he first sat in the car in the paddock on Wednesday afternoon. Then he had been worried about the driving position, something which can prove problematical over ten laps let alone twenty-four hours. For a former Grovewood Award winner with plenty of experience in everything from Clubmens to Formula Atlantic, his comments about that first acquaintance with this most legendary of sports racing machines are worth noting.

"My initial impression was that everything was too close. The steering wheel; the pedals; it was a cramped position. But having driven it I now realise how it is the correct position for a Porsche because they are quite heavy to drive and so it does all make sense. It is absolutely spot on, my only problem being that I have long legs and my right knee continually knocks the wipers on, especially as I go through the Porsche

Curves. Unusually for a racing car they are self cancelling which is all rather good. It goes hand-in-hand with the ignition key and door locks!"

All he would admit to was that he might have preferred slightly different gearing but then only to suit his own particular driving style. Other than that is was a nicely balanced and well set-up motor car. Hans Stuck had once said that driving a Porsche 962 down the Mulsanne was like driving a Mercedes limo on the Champs-Elysees. By the sound of it, Porsche had another convert to the ranks of this classic piece of kit.

"It is not a car to be afraid of, going through all the corners nicely. It is all very predictable. If the tail steps out it's not a problem. There is absolutely no problem with race driving a Porsche, it is just another racing car, but it is a different animal in the sense that it is an ideal Le Mans or Daytona car. No wonder it has got such a good record. The gearbox, for instance, is a much slower change than on a Hewland and while that does not make for a good sprint car, in terms of doing a race like this it is brilliant because it forces you to make the slow changes you should be making even if you had a Hewland. So it must be easier on the transmission and engines."

All that was left was to run the race. It had been both a fun and frustrating few days, the new experience of driving a legend dimmed only by the fact that he had managed less than twenty laps thus far. But as Britain's unsung reigning motorsports world champion –

someone overlooked both in the FISA banquet and BBC TV'S annual 'Sports Personality of the Year' soiree last winter – he was professional enough to know there was a job to be done and that he could do it.

With only so few laps under his belt, not even getting a go in the Warm-Up, through rain or shine, light and dark, Nick Adams was preparing to run at well over 200 miles an hour for as long as it took in his quest for Le Mans honours.

"We are not going to match the Mazdas for pace. The key to their success has always been ultra reliability but at a much lower pace than they are running this year so I would have thought they must now be compromising on reliability. Our game plan is to do late three-fifties/early four minutes and try to do so for twenty-four hours. If we do, who knows. No doubt I will be called upon to do the first double night stint. . . ."

Herr Gebhardt, Signor Moretti and Mister Adams enjoy the pre-race festivities.

THE LONG AND WINDING ROAD

The introduction of chicanes on the Mulsanne Straight was, without doubt, as much for political reasons as safety. It served to show the ACO who really runs the race. FISA.

One, just after the Hunaudieres Restaurant/Bar was right-left. The other, just before the infamous Mulsanne Kink, mirrored it. Originally called L'Arche and La Floriandiere respectively, for commercial considerations they were subsequently renamed Virage Nissan and Virade de la Carte S.

The following are the comments of a random selection of drivers after qualifying. Their responses say a lot about the track and the people who promote, organise, maintain and build it. They also say a lot about the drivers' themselves. . . .

TIM HARVEY (SPICE #21) : "Compared to last year, they have probably brought us five or seven seconds a lap closer to the others without us doing anything because we don't lose so much time down the straight. But this is still a power circuit so not ideally suited to us.

"Overall, I prefer Le Mans with the long straight. That is the nature of the race, made it special, what the magic has all been about. It is still a big event but is now just another track. It has lost that special appeal. It is not one I would like to race on all the time but once a year it was something very special. I am glad I got to race on the old circuit.

"I don't think the strain on the driver is a problem. It is safer in the sense that there is perhaps less likelihood of a tyre blowout, but there is only room for one car in the chicanes and the slower cars are now crossing the road to sweep into the chicanes twice instead of once for The Kink, and the closing speeds are very great. I expect there will be a lot of problems there (in the race) but they will probably be reasonably minor. It is impossible for people to stay out of the way because they are totally committed, doing the best they can and have not got time to look in the mirrors while doing 200mph into a second gear chicane."

FRANZ KONRAD (JAGUAR #2) : "The first is very bumpy which is not so easy for a car in such a long race. There will be a lot of problems for gearboxes and driveshafts and suspension. But they're okay. I feel that it is safer than before."

JAN LAMMERS (JAGUAR #2) : "We do not yet know what the penalty is that we will have to pay for them but first of all it is safer, without a doubt. It puts more stress into the drivers, extra braking and gearchange points, and I think the fact that we have a straight which is much shorter means we can run more aerodynamics whereas before we used little downforce which made the car very light over the bumps which meant it would tend to break traction every now and then. So it is safer on the bumps because we run more aerodynamics and a little extra loading into the car because of the corners so it evens out."

BOB WOLLEK (PORSCHE #9): "Basically, they are a good idea but I don't like it because driving through chicanes is not very interesting. The high speed on the straightaway has always been a problem and with the car going quicker and quicker the problem became bigger and bigger.

"The way they have been built is not fantastic, especially the first one. The second one appears to be much better. The first one is bad, very bumpy. The signalling is bad too.

"Before, the straight was a problem because of the high speed and the accidents. Now the high speed is not the problem any more but the chicanes and the extra gear shifting are. I don't think it puts more strain on the driver. I thought it would but now do not think so. But certainly it is going to be much harder on the car."

MARC DUEZ (PORSCHE #26) : "It is a pity. I understand that we need more safety but they are not built correctly. The first is very bumpy and very difficult to see in the dark. This is not very clever for a twenty-four hour race.

"The long straight was good because you could relax, pass people in safety, but now you have to attack all the time and take risks on braking points. This is not the traditional Le Mans way of driving."

STEVE MILLEN (NISSAN #84) : "I would love to have run down it when it was the full open Mulsanne but Jonathan Palmer's accident would have been very big had he not already had to slow down for a chicane."

NICK ADAMS (PORSCHE #203) : "As chicanes go they are fine but on this circuit they are spoiling a very good straight. Straights in themselves are not interesting but this one was a feature of the circuit. I don't think it has done anything for safety at all, Jonathan Palmer's accident confirming that it would not have been any more severe if the chicanes had not been there. It was still a 200 miles an hour accident and the triple layer guard rails did their job, containing the car within the circuit. On that basis the safety of the circuit was not compromised.

"But they are here and they are alright, the second one better than the first, more interesting. It has a fast entry and tight middle bit, the first one having a tight entry so all you can do is brake and downchange, steer around the wretched thing and toodle out. They are bound to put more strain on drivers and cars, definitely.

"The first one, especially, is not overly illuminated and is hard to pick up. When I got stranded on the first day when the clutch went I watched the rest of the first session from there and four cars missed their breaking points, having to weave their way through the barriers. It's all part of the fun!"

JAMES WEAVER (PORSCHE #43) : "The chicanes basically change the whole complexion of the race because you want a lot more downforce now which means more load into the car and that you have to work a lot harder through the corners.

"In my opinion it has made things worse because Le Mans is all about the Mulsanne and they have taken that away. What you should have had is tyre temperature and pressure sensors on all the cars because punctures are the problem. There are so many gravel traps and people are spraying it everywhere that you're more likely to pick up a puncture driving over all that mugumbo so, generally, I would say 'nil points'!"

WAYNE TAYLOR (PORSCHE #33) : "The chicanes are a little bit tight but I think it's better. You feel a lot safer. The back section going down to Indianapolis is probably more dangerous than Mulsanne was in the first place so they probably should have put a chicane in there too."

Give FISA time, Wayne, give them time. . . .

BRITISH RACING GREENE

Peering out from behind his half-rim spectacles he looks like a learned professor. In his way he is, because if they had first class honours degrees for knowledge and experience of motor racing the man who is acknowledged as probably *the* best team manager around would pass with flying colours.

Keith Greene was born into motor racing. His father, Sid Greene, raced at Brooklands and Donington before becoming a Spitfire pilot during The Second World War – despite the fact he had lost his left arm in an accident when aged sixteen.

Afterwards, having helped start Gilby Engineering and built it up to be a component supplier to the likes of Ford and Frigidaire, he also became well known as a motor racing entrant, Stirling Moss, Mike Hawthorn and particularly Roy Salvadori amongst those benefitting from his patronage. Later there would even be a couple of Gilby cars, designed by Len Terry, one a front engined Climax sports racer, the other a rear engined BRM F.1. machine.

It was in this environment that Keith grew up and soon started racing, taking part in a handful of World Championship Grands Prix and also partnering Alan Stacey in a Lotus XVII at Le Mans in 1959. Although their engine broke in the night with due irony the race was won by an Aston Martin driven by Carroll Shelby and Gilby 'protege' Salvadori.

Keith raced on until the mid-sixties, his reputation being as a consistent rather than rapid pilote, until he came to the point whereby having a wife and child, the company being sold, and the realisation that he was in his own words 'not as good as he hoped he was going to be', he hung up his helmet.

And picked up a clip board. Since then the organisations and teams Keith Greene has been associated with reads like a Who's Who of motor racing. There was Armstrong shock absorbers and Alan Mann Racing, Broadspeed and Brabham. Keith was the one hired by Bernie Ecclestone to run the F.1. team when he purchased it from Ron Tauranac. After that he got involved in John Watson's early G.P. forays with the Hexagon of Highgate operation, the association with the North London quality car emporium also leading to F.5000 and setting up an agency for superbikes, motorcycles being one of his other passions.

After a year working again for Mr.Ecclestone in IRTS, then came a long spell with Gordon Spice not only regarding the winning of umpteen saloon car championships but also the Ford C100 'Le Mans' programme which was controversially terminated early in 1983. Heavily reworked from their previously uninspired form by Tony Southgate, later to design the TWR Jaguars, the cars were due to race with turbocharged Cosworth V8s.

"We had actually completed a couple of tests down at Paul Ricard (with 3.9 litre normally aspirated engines installed) when Stuart Turner came back into the frame as impresario and chopped the lot, including the RS1700T rally car.

"We would have had a 1000bhp available to us from a single turbo, no sweat. We would have won a race in the first year, if not more than one. We had Marc Surer as a driver and various others, Manfred Winkelhock too. We had good mechanics.

"He scrapped I cannot imagine how many million of quids worth of 'gear'. They had all the transaxles for hundreds of cars plus spares already done, everything. We had all our engines, all the gearboxes and spares. The second car was three-quarters built. It was an amazing decision."

"It was an amazing decision."

With the C100 zapped there was nothing left for Keith to do but find some other outlet for his talents. Since then there has been the Porsche teams of John Fitpatrick and Richard Lloyd, partnership with Dave Prewitt in GPM and most recently a year at Nissan Motorsports Europe and now the SARD Toyota attack.

Nor is that all. Spliced in amongst the 'day jobs' have been several short term consultancy posts and other helping hands, the most notable of which was masterminding Jean Rondeau's successful attempt on the Le Mans 24 Hours ten years ago.

There were also consecutive victories for JFR and RLR at Brands Hatch in 1983/84, both noted for their race-winning technical tweaks. Revealing the secrets of those successes, one could be said to have been the result of innnovative thinking, the other of things which go boomp in the night.

"With 'Fitz' it was in the rain. We had a pretty trick piece of kit, some fans operated by the turbos which actually worked very well on the underbody. (They were) totally legal but nobody else had ever thought of it. It was probably a variation of the Jim Hall/Chaparral idea.

"Our chief mechanic, who was an American, had kicked some ideas around and found some industrial fans that we could drive off the turbos. He just thought we could give it a whizz. We did and it worked fine. It did not give us much (of an advantage) but it gave us an edge. As it was wet it was enough for us to walk all over everybody because 'Fitz' was very good and Derek Warwick was brilliant. That combination just shafted the rest of them, it was great."

Downforce is the name of the game. The following year, it was the upstart front wing on the RLR 956 of Jonathan Palmer and Jan Lammers which grabbed all the attention.

"I came up with the idea of the front wing because Brands is always a problem with understeer. It worked 'real brill' with us with Palmer and Lammers. I think we led every lap. That was nice. It's a case of finding edges all the time, isn't it?"

It was not so much a question, more a statement of fact. The logical thing is to assume it was the result of months of hard labour and weeks of wind tunnel evaluation. Wrong.

"I just thought about it in bed one night and went up to Bob Sparshott's and got it made the next day!"

Of such things are legends and victories made. But not all of Keith's associations have been so fruitful. Take the Nissan job at Le Mans in 1986 as a prime example.

"They asked me to be a consultant to them. They wanted the advice but it is very difficult for them to accept it, especially from a westerner.

"They have special divisions and the Engine Division is a very important one. You have also got Engineering and Marketing. Marketing were the people who thought more in a western way and that they should be having some western influence because westerners were quite good at motor racing. In a board meeting type of situation, Marketing won over Engineering because Engineering thought that to not lose face they could do it anyway. And because Marketing won Engineering, maybe, were not co-operative when it came to me arriving (as they could/should have been)."

Never having been afforded the opportunity to go out to Japan to see the programme taking effect, Keith was required to turn up ten days or so prior to the race and influence eighty or so Japanese engineers and mechanics, most of whom spoke little or no English, with his expertise and opinions.

"Engines Division did not want to know about running any proper boost or anything else. In theory, they didn't – until I caught them cheating when it was their drivers in the car. (They were) changing the boost from the agreed figures we were using for James Weaver when he drove, hoping I did not notice. In the end I removed the boost knobs from the dash panels so they could not touch them. And I taped off the microchip as well.

"I then caught them changing the boost on race engines with about twenty minutes to go of last practice. One of the mechanics was in the car twisting the boost knob stems with a pair of stilsons!"

In the consequential conversation with the Nissan hierarchy the no nonsense straight talking for which Greene-san is well known needed no translation.

"They appreciated what I did because it straightened out a lot of things which were typifying the Japanese mentality at that time. They weren't pulling together, there was distrust and were, in certain areas, trying to save their own face. James was three seconds a lap quicker than any of them with the limited boost, limited revs and everything else they gave him. From memory, he was actually on the rev limit before the Restaurant and he'd got three miles (of the old Mulsanne) left!

"The upshot of it was that they did not run the car. I also mentioned a lot of other things, the way Weaver was being treated and so on, so there were a lot of apologies. They obviously appreciated that I was not just being smart-arsed. The way they were behaving WAS bad and I spoke to the main man and he agreed my position."

So much so that when he went to the Fuji race later that year Keith was guest of honour at a special dinner. They also paid him to help out the following year too. And he ran the Nissan Motorsports Europe team under Howard Marsden throughout 1989. Not that his most recent link with the marque ended so amicably.

The way he tells it, the Japanese end of the equation is not the only one which can give problems. Indeed, the difficulties he talks about may well also explain the protracted will they or won't they saga going on as this is written about Nissan's continued involvement or not in WSPC racing.

In his opinion, a lot of the componentry received from Lola was sub-standard and this led to a lot of heated debate, Keith's forthright manner not endearing him to the car constructors and making things uneasy bearing in mind the close working and financial situation between NME and Lola. In the end he did not jump but was pushed, his contract not being renewed.

"I did not drop any clangers and if you look at the history books we did a damned good job for a brand new team with a brand new engine and a brand new car. In Year #1 there aren't many teams in World Championship racing that had the results they had. I was the fall guy, I guess, for saying what was the truth."

Once again Keith found himself looking for work. Although there have been times before when he despaired of getting suitable employment, mainly when people had big ideas but little money – "you cannot spend 'being wanted' at Sainsburys" – this time he did not have too long to wait, the well respected Japanese SARD team realising this was a golden opportunity not to be missed and hiring him to oversee their national championship efforts plus their return to Le Mans for the first time since the early seventies. Nissan one year, Toyota the next, the more things change the more they stay the same.

"The thinking is the same, they have the same sort of attitude (as Nissan) and the same sort of problems, mainly the fuel. Ironically, from the 'Land of the Microchip' it still takes a lot of time to get their act together. It did at Nissan and still is and it is the same sort of situation at Toyota.

"The main difference is that the Toyota is all in-house. Toyota Research and Development supply the cars and the money both to TOMS and SARD and TOMS UK. It makes it easier in the sense that they have immediate control over anything they want to do or change but there is still a lot of people involved in making a decision so you are still in the same basic boat. It is much more by committee than having one designer who is the chief with some draughtsmen underneath him and one guy who is basically the manager of the engine section. It is a Japanese system, a way of doing things.

"They've had a lot of advice, learned a helluva lot and even back to the Nissan March of '86 they do make copious notes and listen. But there are areas which don't tie up with their line of thinking. That is the main difference, problem, whatever you want to call it. There are a lot of people involved with making a final decision. It does make it difficult.

"Last year with NME it was different as it was a British based thing but the politics were still in the background. And final decisions on anything major, particularly financial, did involve a fairly large Japanese fraternity. TOMS UK have, I believe, a little bit of poetic licence but our people at SARD don't have nor do TOMS in Japan. They are *very* integrated with Toyota R & D who dictate the pace.

"It is and can be frustrating at times because if you have been doing it a long time, which I have, there are a number of things you perhaps 'know' are not right or will not work and can save a lot of time, but I can only give my opinion. It is up to them if they use it or not."

That said, with so much experience Keith has a very good idea what it takes to make a winner.

"I reckon there are five elements in racing. The proper money to do the job, a good car, good management, good guys and good drivers. If any of that is missing, forget it, it's off the menu. And you have to start with the money. If you have that you can choose a good car. When you have that guys want to work for you and you get more good guys to drive it. If it all goes together you've got a result.

"But you have got to have a bit of luck too. You make 95% of it but still need to have the rest. If some clown decides to take your line without looking in his mirror boink, you're gone, end of story and that can happen in hour twenty-three, fifteen minutes before the four o'clock finish."

If that is what it takes to make a good team then what are the ingredients needed to become a topline team manager?

"Attention to detail is the strongest answer I can give you, continual attention to detail. A lot of team managers are more into a sort of a profile than detail but it is very easy to put a blazer on and march around with polished nails. Very nice, but I would not be happy doing that.

"One of my failings is probably presentation because as I am not dressed the same as the guys with the Guccis. If I am kneeling down looking underneath a car there is no point scuffing the top of my Gucci shoes. I'd rather have them to go out in the evening after the car has been finished.

"Obviously the number of years I have been doing it we have been through a few problems and you retain the information from them. The guys do the work but I am 'looking' all the time up to when I have to leave the grid. Whenever I am around the car I'm looking and you would be amazed how many things I spot from loose nuts to cracks to cable runs, chaffing of looms or whatever. As good as the guys are there are ten thousand bits on a car and the more experienced eyes which look over it the better."

Besides being the eyes if not the ears of whoever is employing him at the time, there is also the task of keeping everyone happy, the role encompassing everything from ensuring people get fed to being Father Confessor for their troubles and woes.

"A major part of my job is keeping the morale up, sorting out the niggles. It is all part of the package. It is a headache at times; when they have a problem, when you don't get them a tee-shirt. . . ."

Not that anyone can rest on their laurels and reputation. In this game you are only as good as your last race result and Keith Greene knows the rules are altering while the game is still in motion. The times they are a changing.

"Executives in Nissan or Toyota or wherever now look for the specialists. The thirty years of hands-on grass roots way of sorting things out suddenly looks a bit old hat. So, at 52-years old, they might say 'yes he has done very well' and talk about it as past. 'Why don't we try young Guiseppe who is AMI MechE etcetera, 25-years old and give him a whizz for less money?' All of a sudden all your experience in what is now a high-tech industry may go down the tubes."

If that were to happen it could be that Keith would get out of racing altogether. He has had opportunities in the past, amongst them one to partner Alan Mann when he took over Fairoaks Aerodrome, another to go selling boats in the Med. Such a loss is one the sport can ill afford. But in an arena which has the highest of highs and the most deadly of lows his is a well balanced and positive approach to the future, whatever it may bring.

"You wouldn't do it if you didn't enjoy it. It is the same when the weekend has gone bad. The next day you are depressed and the day after you're right into the next programme. You have to be otherwise you would not be in it. History is an hour ago."

Looking out of the top of his half-rims, he smiled that familiar craggy smile. Somebody called; they had a problem with the car. High-tech or low-tech, it did not matter, they wanted help from the best team manager of them all. . . .

The Walkinshaw Wonders! David Leslie, John Nielsen, Price Cobb, Alain Ferte, Michel Ferte, Martin Brundle, Eliseo Salazar, Davy Jones and Luis Perez Sala toe the party line while awaiting the return of Andy Wallace, Franz Konrad and Jan Lammers from the 'Driver Presentation' ceremony.

DAYS OF THUNDER (PART ONE)

"**R**ule Brittania, Brittania Rules Le Mans. . . ."
By Friday lunchtime the party was in full swing. Up at Les Hunaudieres on what tomorrow would be the Mulsanne Straight, if you weren't British you weren't there. Well, almost. Sitting on the straw bales, resting against the armco, as the beer flowed so did the singing, The Purple Army already in both good spirits and good voice.

Coming from every corner of the land, the Heybridge Heroes were already in town as were the Bovis boys and girls. They'd been there since Monday as part of the advance guard. The rest had followed and now their numbers filled every available nook and cranny, every possible vantage point, to capacity.

Down the road apiece from massive speakers their came the sound of a recording of 'The Last Night Of The Proms'. Quadrophonic, graphic equalised, wowed and fluttered, it filled the air and stirred the emotions, fifty thousand 'Brits' about to have a weekend of fun without the mayhem caused a similar number across the continent at the World Cup soccer finals in Italy.

Outside the restaurant a Lagonda stood aloof from the throng, reminding some of the 'good old days', others of the sudden and disappointing demise of the Aston Martin team which had done them so proud twelve months ago. When the owner finally fired up its massive motor and pulled off into the traffic in a roar or sound and a rejoice of vision once and for all it silenced those inane questions, spoken or unsaid, as to whether it was real or not, mister.

Almost at the same time as it did so, unnoticed by all but a vigilant few three times winner Phil Hill, America's first World Champion, slipped his small white Peugeot out from the dirt road opposite and headed in the other direction.

Heroes of yesteryear, tomorrow would bring new ones. But today was one for seeing and being seen, of fun and relaxation. For all but the teams tonights party would go on until late. . . .

Reflecting on a glorious past, Bentley were part of the pre-race hullabaloo.

They're Off! Bailey and Larrauri lead the way.

Saturday dawned decidedly brighter than the rest of the week had been, the elements obviously fuelled by the prospect of an exciting battle ahead. By the time of the aptly named Warm-Up the sun was already high in an almost cloudless sky.

For most of the teams the session passed without major incident but down at Nissan they were in double trouble, their #25 car suffering a slipping clutch and gearbox problems, the #83 version needing its bag tank replaced when a fuel leak was discovered. Things were starting to go wrong for those who had hogged most of the headlines so far. Next door at TWR the mood was much more upbeat as Brundle topped the times, the other three XJRs all in the first six. It was looking good for Jag.

An accident at the very start of the Renault support race delayed things awhile, giving Nissan and anyone else who needed it valuable extra time to complete their repairs. Two drivers were injured in the melee, Oscar Larrauri shaken but otherwise unhurt. Why the front row man was risking his all in this sideshow was not apparent but by the following morning the consequences would be.

When everything finally settled down eventually the cars were pushed out onto the track and lined up in their customary angled fashion as the drivers went through the standard procedure of being introduced to the crowd, last first. All except Cudini, Laffite and Stuck, that is, who were racing saloons at the Nurburgring before jetting back to France that evening. Awaiting their turn, it did not need any orchestration from the Jaguar drivers to get the biggest cheers yet spurred on by the likes of Price Cobb, the Colorado based Texan revelling in the atmosphere of the most famous motor race on earth, there was no doubting who were the favourites if the unofficial cheerometer was anything to go by.

In sharp contrast, despite containing two fast 'Brits' the reception given to the pole sitting car was at best polite, by comparison almost non-existant. In the pre-race war of nerves it was one up to the Jags.

And one down to Hawaiian Tropic. That there was no flypast by the 'Patrouille de France' went almost unnoticed. That there were no parachutists, ditto. But the sight – or lack of one – of the Hawaiian Tropic girls was almost too much to bear. The Takefuji nymph might have been cute and the traditionally attired Mazda ladies likewise, but the brown bikinied maidens were sorely missed. Sacre bleu! Is nothing sacred?

When the pre-race festivities were over and done with the cars took up their positions on the two by two grid which stretched the whole length of the Pits Straight, forty-nine gleaming and powerful chargers ready for the off. In another break 'with the tradition of recent years, there would be no WM waiting to start from the pitlane when all the rest had gone. . . .

Slowly they moved away, the pair of Nissan 300SX pace cars heading them around, returning half a minute early but not soon enough for poor Kenny Acheson who had only gotten as far as Arnage before being overwhelmed by all manner of problems, the repairs carried out since its Warm-Up dramas not lasting much more than four miles let alone twenty-four hours. Brakes, gearbox, transmission; you name it and Nissan #25 seemed to be suffering from it. The race had not yet begun but already the pendulum of good fortune had swung away from the Japanese.

Alistair Fenwick's Tiga was the first pits visitor but would survive to make the finish.

Julian Bailey, however, was trying to make up the deficit. As everyone jostled for position through the Ford Chicane the pace cars peeled right and left the stage to the stars of the show. To the customary cheer from the assembled throng, Bailey floored the accelerator and the pole car accelerated hard past the grandstands and away, only Larrauri seeming to give chase.

Oscar feinted to go inside him at the first corner but thought better of it, the multi-hued Repsol 962 settling for becoming almost attached to the Nissan's hind quarters as the pair made their way under the Dunlop Bridge through the Esses and sharp right around Tertre Rouge.

Gearboxes are traditionally the thing that gives most trouble at Le Mans and the new circuit layout would only enhance that fear. For sure, most pundits reckoned the transmission to be the Nissan weak link, if any, a feeling given weight by what had already happened to Acheson. And without a doubt Larrauri looked keen to give the item the very closest of inspections as nine-point-six metres of high speed high-tech headed out down Mulsanne for the first time in anger, the two as one

and already a hundred yards clear of the rest.

Forty thousand unleashed horses in a whirlwind of speed and light. Two more Nissans held the next pair of places, Jelinski fifth, Jaguars in sixth, seventh and eighth. By the time they got to the first chicane Jelinski had muscled his way into fourth. By the time they reached the second aberration the Minolta Toyota was splitting the Jaguars, John Nielsen in the #3 car happy to bide his time in the early going, not wishing to get into any early contretemps as he had done during both the last two years. The Kenwood Porsche rounded out the top ten as they

. . . nine-point-six metres of high-speed high-tech . . .

turned Mulsanne Corner and headed for home.

All the way around the rest of the lap Larrauri hustled Bailey, the leader driving impeccably to maintain his slight advantage. By the time they completed the first tour of the French countryside the pair were three hundred yards up on their pursuers and putting on a show. With Davy Jones having demoted Geoff Brabham another spot at Indianapolis the first lap leader board read Nissan, Porsche, Nissan, Porsche, Jaguar, Nissan, Jaguar, Toyota, Jaguar, Porsche. What many claimed to be the most open Le Mans for years was certainly starting that way.

As the remainder of the field filed past it was obvious that Jan Lammers was on the move, already up to twelfth and making nonsense of his lowly starting spot. Further back, the Lancia had the temerity to drive inside Tim Lee-Davey as they came past the pits for the first time, the Porsche driver gathering up his pride and place before the next corner. Last, a full two miles down on the leaders, came the lonely Tiga, the car sounding rough and due to become the first pitstopper next time around. Somebody has to be.

Nissan #83 led the chase on behalf of the Japanese contingent. Alas to no avail.

Onto the second lap and Brabham was trying to fight back, Jelinski just to hold on, his tyres already proving unequal to the task. Jones kicked up the dust as he looked for a way past the ailing Porsche, fourth through to ninth nose-to-tail as they headed down Mulsanne for the second time. Spinning wildly backwards, Jurgen Laessig in a Primagaz Porsche became the first visitor the kitty-litter. He would not be the last.

Instead of going up, Brabham went down, Lees demoting him seconds after Brundle had, the NPTI Nissan now eighth. A wily campaigner wise beyond his years, Geoff was another who was not out to try winning a twenty-four hour race in the first twenty-four minutes. Jones then took Jelinski to end Lap2 in fourth. Up at the front 'Jules' was doing a great job holding 'Popi' at bay, thereby going someway to expunge the embarrassment of '89 when his demon start ended so ignominiously after only a handful of laps. Keeping it firmly on the island as the Porsche tried every which way past, oh what a difference a year makes.

Lap 3 and once again the ingredients were mildly stirred, the front pair a quarter mile clear of the rest, Nissan #23 leading Jones, leading Jelinski, Brundle, Nielsen et al. Lees was eighth, Brabham ninth, the last of the Silk Cut cars now in tenth. Mazda #202 headed GTP, the Lombardi Spice taking C2 honours. Only towards the end of the fourth tour did Bailey roll off the throttle and let Larrauri by, tucking in to his slipstream a few lengths back.

With the Porsche now out in front things started to stabilise. Despite the fact that Oscar was being as spectacular as ever the pair were no longer pulling away from their pursuers at the rate they previously had for now they were in amongst the back markers. By letting Larrauri be first on the scene, Bailey was allowing the Repsol car to be the one who came of worst if someone ahead was not paying close attention to their mirrors. Bailey could let the 962 do all the hard work yet be handily placed to capitalise on any misfortune. If there had been a prize for the Most Improved Driver thus far, the former Tyrrell F.1. man would have been a prime contender.

Pitstops were starting to play their part too, Raphanel heading Toyota #38 up the lane after only nineteen minutes with braking problems while the second IMSA-run Nissan, started by Bob Earl, came in shortly afterwards to report a water leak, the first of what would be a whole catalogue of woes. Both were soon on their way again but would be back before much longer, the SARD machine losing more time after its nosecone disappeared, the NPTI car when the temperature guage hit the red once more. Less than half an hour gone and already their hopes of a good result were all but dashed, the prospect of running around for twenty-four hours at that point seeming more like twenty-four days.

Another early visitor was Cohen-Oliver in the second Davey 962, 'Banzai Max' losing a wheel as he arrived at the Ford Chicane but able to make his way straight in for a replacement, the errant BBS bouncing high and harmless into the gravel.

More serious were the burdens of Frank Jelinski, the pre-race favourite Porsche soon coming in for fresh rubber in the hope it would solve its problems. It didn't. Despite the attentions of the factory's finest, soon Joest's top gun would be sixteenth.

Wollek wasn't having much fun either, the dark blue of his Mizuno livery reflecting his mood as he struggled to keep the best of the Toyotas in sight, the Joest team's third car (started by Pescarolo) way back in the pack out of immediate contention. It was going to be an uphill task if the 'works' Porsches were to pull this one out of the bag.

Bailey handed over to Blundell, Larrauri stayed aboard. When all was said and done Repsol #16 had a few seconds cushion on the field, Mark closing it down with ease so that after the first hour there was still only a couple of lengths between them. In an effort to stay on terms Blundell could be seen running very wide and riding the kerbs on both sides of Tertre Rouge, the Porsche throwing up sand in his face in an attempt to break the tow. It was very spectacular stuff.

Behind them the Jaguars were almost in formation, Hasemi's NISMO Nissan having dwindled to eighth after its pitstop, only Brabham still in the fight in fifth despite a quick spin at the first turn, his attention apparently having been distracted by a car leaving the pitlane. Third and fourth, sixth and seventh, it was already looking promising for Major Tom.

At the next round of stops Pareja took up the challenge for the Brun equipe but being unable to match his team leader's pace soon the Nissan was by, an ever widening gap developing between them. With fifteen minutes left of the second hour it had drifted out to thirty-one seconds, Brundle only four more in arrears. Five minutes later and the Englishman was past. When team owner Brun later came to take his first turn behind the steering wheel he would prove slower still, the car dropping out of the top half a dozen while Larrauri rested.

With three hours down it was now David Leslie who held second aboard Silk Cat #1, the Cumbrian domiciled Scot doing a very fine job in his opening race stint as a 'works' Jag driver, the Brabham/Daly/Robinson Nissan third. Three more XJR-12s were filling the next trio of places through to sixth.

Further down the order others were going great guns too, notably the Alpha Porsche of Needell/Reid/Sears, already as high as tenth. Fitted with Yokohamas and the high downforce and short tail arrangement as per the Repsol 962, it was proving an inspired combination. Kremer also had Yokohamas but the difference made by running in *langheck* form would ultimately tell, neither ever being on the full pace of the race.

By now the sun was beginning to dip behind the grandstands, the long hot day giving way to a long not-quite-so-hot evening. As much of the crowd drifted away to their revelries the smell of hot frites and garlic saucisses and other culinary disasters rent the air. France may be the home of good food but Le Circuit de la Sarthe is to gastronomie what Tom Walkinshaw is to ballet dancing.

Three wheels on his wagon, Max Cohen-Olivar loses a left front fortunately while already en route to the pits.

The Joest 962 of Bell/Jelinski/Stuck did not live up to its hoped-for form in the early going due to tyre and brake problems.

JULIAN BAILEY (NISSAN #24) : "I had to let Larrauri past because he wanted to play while I had to drive to our fuel schedule. But we are back in front now so it didn't hurt to lose the lead for a few laps."

GEOFF BRABHAM (NISSAN #83) : "Somebody came out of the pits and distracted me. I left my braking too late and slid off. I figure the Jaguars are our biggest threat so am just tagging along with them."

RAY MALLOCK (NISSAN TEAM) : "We cannot show too much excitement about our position on the track because it is still early in the race. What is important is that we are on schedule and just happen to be leading at the moment!'

The drop in temperature was helping some more than others, the Brabham/Daly/Robinson R90C one of those who seemed to benefit most in the cool evening air, moving into second place behind its sister car, Brancatelli now at the wheel of the leader as the fourth hour passed into the history books. Third through sixth ran the Jaguars, unhurried and unflustered, maintaining a pace they felt sure they could win with. Just like at Daytona.

In the Florida classic a few months before Porsche had set the early pace only to fade away, the journey into the night a running battle between TWR and the Nissans. Here it was starting to take on a similar pattern. Down in the Jaguar enclave nobody was saying much just yet, remaining quietly optimistic, knowing all they could now hope for was more of the same – preferably without all the late drama.

One of the incidents Jaguar had benefited from back then was when the leader had struck a backmarker, crippling its effort in one moment of disaster. Not quite deja vu, nevertheless when 'Branca' hurtled inside Aguri Suzuki's twelfth placed Toyota at the Dunlop Curve you had the feeling that the Gods of Racing were replaying an old script. The left front corner of the Nissan clipped the right rear section of the Taka-Q entry and before anyone could blink the Larrousse F.1. pilote was over the tyre wall and into the armco, the barrier laid flat at 170 miles an hour. It was a very heavy impact, a HUGE accident, one from which it took Suzuki more than a few moments to recover his senses, finally being helped from the wreckage by the corner marshalls. He had been very lucky. Not so the chassis, yet another Toyota tub headed for that great scrapyard in the sky. How many was that so far this season? Five?

Brancatelli was more fortunate, the impact only ripping off the left front wing and puncturing the tyre. Slowly he made his way around to the pits for repairs, Bailey taking over. In the Press Centre, the pits marshall's report caused more than a modicum of amusement stating as it did that the repairs had been effected due to 'a slight accident'. Obviously not one to be easily over-awed, the same guy would probably have classified the coming together of the Titanic and a certain large lump of ice as 'a minor collision'. . . .

With the erstwhile leader now relegated to sixth as a result of its misadventures, Brabham and Friends led from Brundle & Co., the Jaguar men getting ahead at pit stops. In third, Price Cobb and John Nielsen were also doing an excellent job while one lap down and climbing back, Repsol #16 was once more in the very capable hands of Oscar Larrauri who was taking the fight to anybody who cared to cross his path. Fourth after five hours to split the XJRs, as dusk became darkness Brun Motorsport's ongoing challenge to all those factory teams was proving to be one of the highlights of the race.

The lights were now coming on all around the circuit, the musty yellow of pitlane in sharp contrast to the gaudy

spectrums of the fairground, the irridescent glow of trackside marker boards reflecting brightly in the piercing beams of the race cars.

Alas, for some, the night would be one of doom and gloom, the Harvey/Hodgetts/Velez Spice #21 already losing considerable track time with a broken exhaust, this only a prelude to not one but a pair of gearbox rebuilds. Only on Sunday afternoon would the 3½ litre/750 kilo machine make it back into the top twenty. Following on from their problems of last year, if this is supposed to be good experience for the new era, they were certainly learning the hard way. Nor did it bode well for the race of 1992. If there is a race in '92, that is.

Both the Kremer cars were also spending more than the preferred amount of time stationary, the Davey 962s also becoming regular features of pitlane. As were the Schuppan pair, broken exhausts the main bete-noir of the High Wycombe team. Despite their combined problems, all six would get to the finish, albeit way down the 'Resultat Final'. For a beleaguered Tim Lee-Davey, in particular, that would be a triumph in itself.

Even the normally reliable Mazdas were suffering unexpectedly, all three of them in such disarray that they were letting the Momo Porsche get away with the GTP class. So much for the predictions that Le Mans' longest served Japanese entrant would get a car into the top five. At this rate they would be lucky to make the top two dozen.

And the pole position car was also in trouble again. Barely an hour after Brancatelli's heave-ho with Suzuki, Bailey pitted with a puncture to the right rear tyre. Dismayed yet undeterred, once resolved without further ado Blundell showed that there was not much wrong with Nissan #24 a little luck would not cure when he set the fastest lap of the race thus far (at 3m40.26s) to begin the long climb back up the leader board, the race still a long way from being settled.

Opposite locking on the opposite page, Oscar Larrauri in typical pose.

Brancatelli came off best after his altercation with the Taka-Q Toyota, winning by a technical knock-out.

SILK CUT
JAGUAR
CREW
Silk Cut
JAGUAR
SILK CUT
JAGUAR
CREW
Castrol
3
SILK CUT
SilkCut
JAGUAR

Nor were Jaguar immune from their share of little gremlins. Price Cobb, for one, had also been in difficulties. Ten minutes into his latest stint a brake problem had seen him take to the gravel at the Chicane L'Arche, kicking more stones onto the roadway and flat spotting the tyres. Stopping for new rubber, the pit crew could find nothing obviously wrong and he was sent out again although at no time thereafter did they inspire much confidence in the drivers. They would need to race accordingly.

Alain Ferte was another for whom fortune chose not to smile on, at least for a while. At just around quarter distance, he had returned to the pits only a few laps into his stint. Water was added and the car went on its way again without further ado. Half an hour later he was back again.

The swirl pot had cracked, leaking away vital fluid. Electing to replace rather than attempt to fix it, soon the Frenchman was back in the fray only to reappear for a third time a few minutes later to have the hoses retightened. In all Jaguar #1 had forfeited four laps to this irritating but vital problem, enough to drop it from second to twelfth in the tight packed order. Although it would run like clockwork for the rest of the night the damage had already been done.

As for the other two, in both instances the handling had 'gone off' slightly, adding to the extra fatigue being imposed on them and everybody else by the Mulsanne chicanes. Not that the drivers were complaining too much, mind you, all fully aware that they were amongst the lucky ones, almost everybody else having suffered far worse fates than they.

When the ACO posted the midnight bulletin, the 'Brabham' Nissan still led, now a minute up on the Cobb/Nielsen XJR. One lap back came Larrauri, then Wallace, then Jones. Brancatelli was again at the wheel of the fastest of the Japanese brigade, in sixth, Hoshino handling its most circumspect in seventh. Alpha were eighth, the three Joest cars mixed in with David Leslie filling the positions ninth through to twelfth.

Momo continued to head up the IMSA class, Nick Adams doing a stirring double night stint to keep them ahead of the screaming Mazdas. Sadly for him and all involved it would all come to nothing two hours later when a broken crownwheel-and-pinion stranded team co-owner Gunther Gebhardt out on the circuit. Porsches don't break crownwheel-and-pinions. This one had.

As for C2, the PC Spice was going like a train. Fourth after the first hour, it now found itself with four laps in hand over the Chamberlain entry, nine ahead of ADA, Mako another two in arrears. Having seen off the early charge of the continentals, it looked for all the world like (probably) the last ever big time outing for the class would be a wholly British affair.

Big cars; little cars; the battered and the bewildered. Onwards into the black they ran at two hundred miles an hour and more, the pace hardly slackening, the shrill pitch of their engines as keen as ever.

BERTRAND GACHOT (MAZDA #202) : "I suddenly found myself without headlights and it was a real shock so I put myself immediately behind another car and followed it into the pits. To make sure I was seen by other cars I produced an almost constant procession of flashes from the exhaust by playing with the throttle. It was a pity because we were beginning to have real fun and go really fast."

NICK ADAMS (PORSCHE #230) : "When I went out on the double night stint we were two laps behind the leading Mazda which must have had problems because I certainly did not overtake it three times even though I was managing to go around ten seconds a lap quicker than my team mates. But when I came back in at about 1.30 in the morning we were one lap ahead. Then Gunther went out and did 1½ stints before coming in to say 'the gearbox is kaput'. The pinion had gone. It was a sad end."

VOLKER WEIDLER (MAZDA #202) : "I was right behind a Toyota, flat in fifth at 300 kph as it passed a slower car, the Lancia. The driver suddenly saw the Toyota as he turned in, swerved and plunged some fifty metres into the trees. I was flat out in fifth on the back straight when it happened and had to go onto the grass to avoid the other cars."

Suddenly one of their number was missing. Out on more than simply a Sunday morning drive, the much delayed Lancia was making its way along from Mulsanne, Fabio Magnani minding his own business down in forty-second place. Twenty-six rungs up the lap charts, Masanori Sekiya was intent on improving things for Toyota, the Minolta car making considerably better progress in the cooler air of the night than it had done earlier and starting to make inroads into the lead of those immediately ahead. The brows are blind just there, down to Indianapolis and Arnage. They are also flat in fifth. Never likely to set the world on fire with its race results, the Lancia was about to come fairly close to doing so with what happened next.

When the startled Magnani looked in his mirrors it was already too late. Cresting the rise behind him like a monster with the devil in its eyes, all he saw was a blinding flash of light. A nudge; a squeal of tyres; a car out of control; in an instant all hell broke loose and the Italian was rolling end over end, demolishing the armco and hurtling into the forest beyond at very high speed.

For a while a strange and ominous silence descended upon the scene, the same eerie chill which had accompanied the not knowing when Win Percy had gone missing in 1987, when Jo Gartner had not come around twelve months earlier.

That same ill wind was also blowing gently down pitlane. When news finally came through of Magnani's miraculous escape a huge collective sigh went up and full focus returned to the job in hand. The third big accident of the week, he too was very fortunate to escape with minor injuries, the conflagration which resulted from his fearful flight destroying not only what was left of the inverted car but some of the trees in which the wreck had landed. They don't come much closer than that.

The accident brought the pace cars out, thereby giving everyone some welcome respite. Ever since the start the race had been unrelenting and the new Mulsanne layout had put in question everyone's stamina and fuel calculations, many a seasoned campaigner suggesting that there would be a lot of cars running dry long before the end. It may have been only a quarter of an hour but it helped, everyone positive that it would benefit them, nobody concerned that it also benefit their rivals.

Someone not so pleased would have been Chip Robinson, the former IMSA champion handling the NPTI Nissan with great style but seeing the advantage he fought so hard to protect all but vanish as the field bunched up behind the pace cars. Somebody else not overly happy for entirely different reasons was Davy Jones, Silk Cat #4 dropping to eighth when a sticking throttle proved awkward to cure, two laps lost in the process. With the winners usually those who have raced hard and fast without fault, already that was the second Jaguar to be temporarily delayed and the race was not yet half run.

Tucking in just in front of the Brundle/Leslie/Alain Ferte car, nor would it have gone unnoticed by TWR that immediately ahead of Jones ran the Joest #7 of Bell/Jelinski/Stuck. While the outcome still favoured Nissan or Jaguar, or just maybe the Repsol 962, nobody could discount these three heroes who were fast making their presence increasingly felt.

'Stucky' and his mates edged closer still soon afterwards when Brancatelli had linkage problems, the gearbox going the whole hog an hour later when it apparently seized on Bailey as he attempted to rejoin the race after taking over from the luckless Italian. When the mechanics eventually went to collect their stricken beastie one climbed aboard, fired it up, selected a gear and calmly drove off. . . .

. . . a strange and ominous silence descended on the scene . . .

It was at 02H18 precisely, as the NPTI 'Brabham' Nissan sat at rest having its steel brake discs replaced, that the Cobb/Nielsen XJR swept by and into the lead. Ahead for the first time other than during the routine pit stop sequences, with an absence of cloud cover the warmth of the day had long since gone and brought behind it the coldest of nights, yet down in the TWR pits and amongst their many fans who were determined to see the vigil through, there was a warm and contented glow of satisfaction of a job well done. So far.

Jaguar had hit the front by running at the pace they had carefully calculated and stuck to, the strategy of Messrs. Walkinshaw, Silman and Dowe working like a treat, especially on the IMSA crewed car aboard which Price Cobb put in a stunning double stint. They had done the easy bit. All they now had to do was keep there for another fourteen hours!

Then thirteen, then twelve. By the time everyone got to half distance the Jaguar had edged just a little clear of the Nissan, the gap small yet significant after all that amount of racing. TWR USA versus NPTI; Tony Dowe against Don Devendorf; Jag-wah fighting Neesan; it was just like an IMSA race, the two teams a credit to the American racing series as they vied for the lead of the greatest sports car race on Earth. TWR reckoned they had something in hand; NPTI reckoned they had something in hand; it was like a couple of prize fighters biding their time as each of them waited to land what they hoped would be the knock-out punch.

Not that it was a fight only between the pair of them. Pareja and Brun were responding magnificently to the fine example shown by Larrauri and were now fully into the swing of things and doing a splendid job to keep the Repsol car in touch. Trading third place with Jaguar #2, with every passing lap the Brunmobile gained a whole host of new friends and everyone knew that Porsche being Porsche, while it maintained its vigil and speed nobody could write off the chances of an upset occurring.

The 'works' Spice C1 battled on bravely, its data acquisition exercise eventually netting eighteenth overall.

DAYS OF THUNDER (PART TWO)

As the race entered its second phase the party was in full swing. Over at the fairground the fat ladies and strippers were strutting their stuff, the dodgems more dangerous than anything seen trackside. In the bierkellers of 'Le Village' they were dancing and shouting, drinking and drinking some more. Oompah bands vied with rugby songs, the sound of the merriment all but blocking out the urgent roar of the racers as they passed by mere yards away. And everywhere there were people, people and more people, those who were still going strong filling every vantage point, those who had wilted under the pressure curled up wherever the fancy took them. The civilised took to their cars, the others anywhere. You would step over them in the passageways, by pass them in corners.

Down in the pits it was, as they say, the same but different. Running the full length of pitlane immediately behind the dugouts there is a dimly lit corridor. Narrow, high walled and noisy, it is a place of respite from the mayhem and dangers just beyond. Motor racing's equivelent of the trenches of the Somme, the loose stone floor is a haven for any mechanic allowed the luxury of a few precious moments of rest, awaiting the next call to arms.

Some just curled up where they fell, immediately at peace with the world. Others had some comforts from home, making the best of camping chairs set onto the uneven surface as if going on a picnic. Up by the Mazda section they were cooking rice with something, down by Team Le Mans – whose privately entered Nissan R89C would soon stop with terminal engine problems having never featured on the leader board – they were cooking something with rice. The less adventurous had to be content with sandwiches. Most would have settled for a warm and comfortable bed. . . .

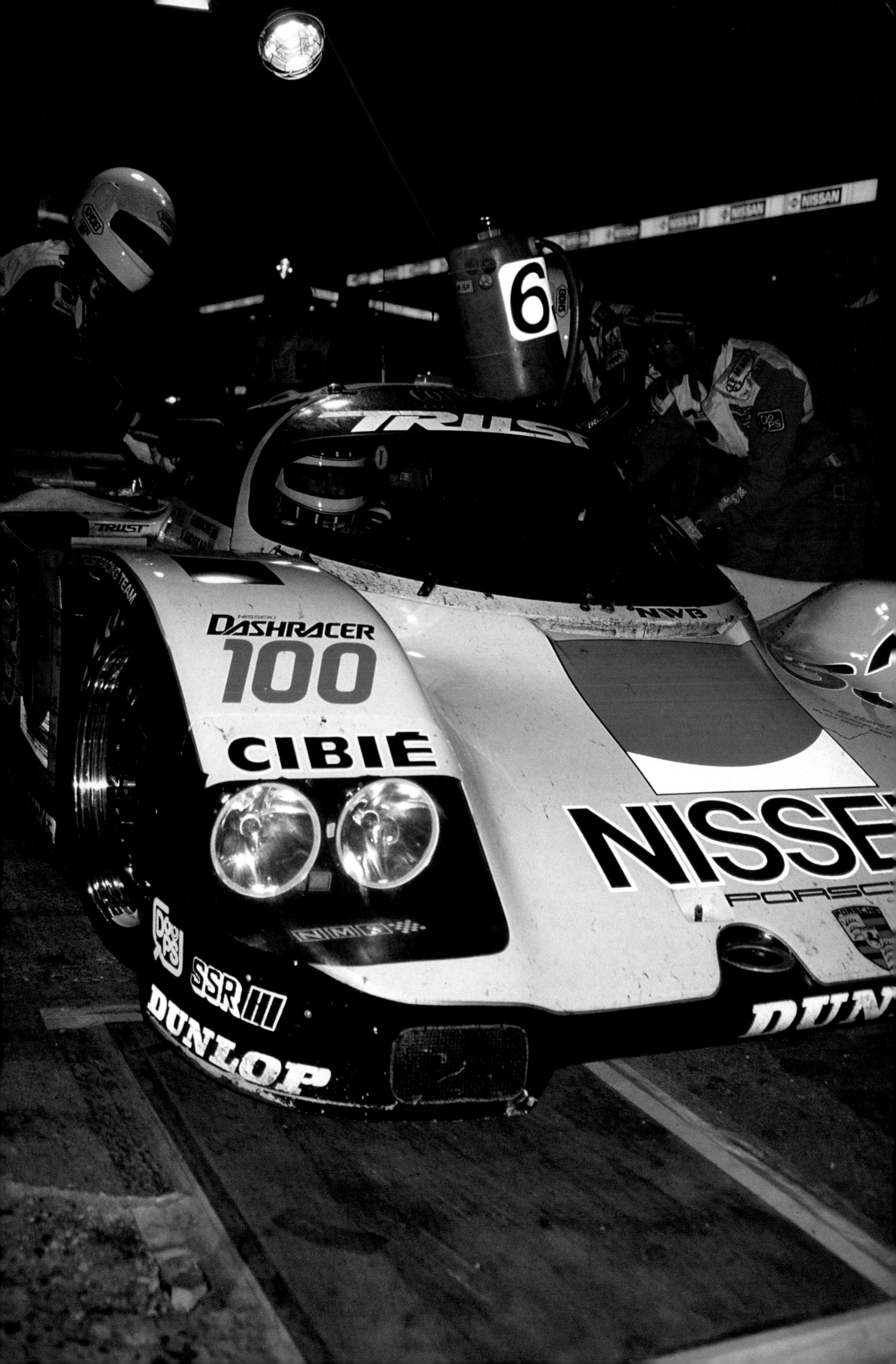
NISSAN
6
TRUST
DASHRACER
100
CIBIÉ
NISSE
SSR
DUNLOP

Out on the track, although wide awake James Weaver was locked into his own private nightmare.

The RLR cars had been, in a word, disappointing. The #44 long tail of Berg/Giacomelli/Watson had been thwarted by wheel bearing and brake problems. A lowly eighteenth, eventually it would struggle home eleventh.

The #43 machine sporting the high downforce short tail a' la Repsol and Alpha, and piloted by 'Gentleman Jim', was having a much better time of it – or would have been had it not suffered problems with brakes and tyres. Only recently, the team had been required to resort to that age old remedy of pouring Coca-Cola over the clutch in order to prevent more troubles. From tenth on the first hour's official time sheets it now showed sixteenth despite some very solid effort by its highly talented driving force which also included JJ Lehto and Manuel Reuter.

At shortly before five-thirty, the loquacious Weaver had been hurtling down through Indianapolis when a sudden deflation of the left rear Goodyear almost sent him into a spin. A flint picked up at the rubble strewn Mulsanne chicanes was suspected to be to blame, his prophesy about the mugumbo come true.

Gathering the pink Porsche up without hitting anything, it was then either a matter of leaving the stricken beast by the roadside or attempting to get back to the sanctuary of pitlane for a replacement. True to his calling, the man behind the wheel elected to make it a case of 'Home James, And Do Spare The Horses'. Cruising in, he radioed the RLR crew of his impending arrival, the mechanics ready and waiting with fresh rubber as his headlamps became discernible at the far end of the pits entry and getting ever closer.

. . . the whole rear end of the Porsche exploded in a circle of flame.

Suddenly, without warning, the whole rear end of the Porsche exploded in a circle of flame. Flailing rubber had ripped off a turbo pipe, hot oil now ignited by the sparks emanating from the down-to-earth corner, the scene one of a huge Catherine Wheel of fire and destruction. All the way up the still crowded roadway came the stricken car, James anxious to get out yet fully aware that if he upped the speed too much he might lose control and cause a mighty accident. Well and truly ablaze, the flames reached up as if to lick the chins of those still watching from the pitlane balcony, the heat melting composite and metal alike. It was a desperate situation.

Fortunately, he made it. Sliding to a stop in its rightful place, no sooner was the car at rest than the driver out, a host of extinguishers pouring their contents towards the target zone to fill the air with a mixture of acrid smoke and chemicals. Finally, they got it under control, RLR #43 then being pushed away into ignominious retirement.

And all the while the chaos had been going on around them, the Alpha team in the adjacent pit to RLR went about a routine stop, unflustered and unhindered, the all-British trio led by Tiff Needell now up into eighth. In more ways than one, it was a wonderful advertisement for mind over matter.

When the sun finally appeared still the Jaguar held a slim advantage over the NPTI Nissan, the pressure never relenting, fully in the knowledge that one false move could wreck it all. And still the Repsol Brun had third, the car going better for longer than anyone could have ever have anticipated, its progess thus far equally a source of joy and embarrassment to the factory personnel attending the 'works' Joest team who could themselves not better sixth. In between, the Japanese crewed NISMO Nissan was still showing everybody what reliability could bring, the car having yet to miss a beat as it held a strong fourth only three laps in arrears. Fifth came the Brundle/Ferte/Leslie XJR, its impressive progress through the night having made up one lap but no more.

Franz Konrad, meanwhile, had decided to crash test the tyre wall at the first chicane. Repairs to the damaged door and broken nose took five laps to complete, dropping it Jaguar #2 to seventh. Those five laps which would make all the difference come flag fall.

As for the fourth Jaguar, the 'Jones' car suffered its own little escapade when co-driver Michel Ferte wounded the nose box while kerb hopping at high speed. Indeed, only the Cobb/Nielsen version seemed immune from any such dramas. All the guys and gals cheering for the purple and white crossed their fingers and started to pray.

True to form, just after dawn TWR lost a car to the gremlins.

By now the crowds were drifting back, the wide and sandy litter strewn terraces opposite the pits beginning to fill. The biggest concentration marked out their territory opposite the Jaguar enclave, the Purple Army preparing for the final hours as the smell of breakfast drifted on the warm fresh morning air. Invigorating those who had made it through the night, although the heart said the worst was over the mind knew that there was still a long way left to run.

Not so for Jaguar #1. True to form, just after dawn TWR lost a car to the gremlins. Every year it happens. In 1986 it was Schlesser's puncture, since then it has been engine or gearbox problems.

This year was no exception despite the fact that the reason was an unusual one, a water pump belt having broken. Fitted into the front of the V12 where it recesses into the back of the chassis the part is nigh on impossible to fix in situ. At 07H30 they pushed the fifth place car away.

One down, three to go. Then two-and-a-half. Then two. While the team elected to transfer Brundle to the #3 car, Eliseo Salazar finally got to drive, switching seats to oust Perez-Sala from the 'Jones' machine. Unfortunately, he did not bring it much luck, Silk Cat #4 soon slipping down the order with its ongoing overheating problems until finally stopped forever shortly after midday when the engine expired under the strain. It was eleventh at the time.

The strain of a long night begins to show on TW. (Above)

Sunday morning and a Porsche charges on, the ADA a victim of the night.

One down and three to go, Jaguar got their customary breakfast time indigestion as Silk Cat #1 expired with engine problems.

Yet if life was getting tense chez TWR it was getting downright traumatic next door at Nissan.

It is customary for teams to station people in the pits of their rivals so as to get an eye witness account of what the state of play is thereabouts. Not so much spies as observers, they then report back, their own team using the information to help plan race strategy. 'The Whizzbang Special has got a damaged sprockel duffling' goes the call. 'Oh, deary me. What spiffing bad luck' comes the riposte. Or something like that. The worse the calamity, the more your own people will be pleased with the news. This isn't sport, this is business.

TWR must have been bordering on unbridled ecstacy! At 07H34, shortly after Jaguar had seen the demise of the 'Brundle' car and already aware of the likely fate of the 'Jones' XJR, the metronome run of the Hasemi/Hoshino/Suzuki car had come to a temporary halt, its first unscheduled stop so far. Broken rear shock absorbers had damaged its rear bodywork requiring both matters to be attended to urgently. Two laps were lost in the process. The cracks were beginning to show.

Worse still, the second placed car was in even bigger trouble. Chip Robinson had already stopped during an earlier episode to complain that he could smell fuel in the cockpit. Nothing was found amiss and he went on his way, eventually handing over as per normal to Derek Daly. Less than an hour later, having just started the second period of his double stint, the Irishman was back, his race suit soaked in petroleum spirit.

The fuel cell, fitted on Saturday morning to replace the one which had come apart at the seams during the Warm-Up, had itself developed a fault. Borrowing a spare from NME, despite slipping out of contention with every minute they stayed immobile, to their eternal credit the team then spent best part of two hours attempting to get their charge into a safe state to return to the race. Sadly, to no avail. Just before eleven o'clock they pushed the NPTI car away for good. It had completed one more lap than last year.

JAMES WEAVER (PORSCHE #43) : "With the ACO planning to knock the pits down before next year's race, I could have saved them a bit of money by parking it next to someone I didn't like!"

DAVID LESLIE (JAGUAR #1) : "We were doing so well but are not so close, it's a long way from seven o'clock in the morning until the finish. There's always next time."

GEOFF BRABHAM (NISSAN #83) : "We had by far the best car and could just run with the leaders or pull away whenever we wanted to. We felt we had everyone handled, no problem. Unfortunately, little things put you down."

STEVE MILLEN (NISSAN #84) : "I am happy about being credited with the fastest lap, for sure. It was set on race boost and the normal tyres, nothing special, so I am very pleased. I was doing a lot of really quick laps early in the morning and one was a really good one."

Nissan saw their hopes dashed when the fuel tank split on the 'Brabham' car. (Opposite)

Lloyd Porsche #44 overcame the fiery demise of its sister car to claim eleventh.

Joest were having a hard time of it, the all-French crew of Laffite/Pescarolo/Ricci taking a disappointing fourteenth.

Steve Millen's new lap record proved there was nothing wrong with Nissan #84 a little reliability would not have done wonders for.

With the only other Nissan still out there, the much delayed #84 car, down in twenty-seventh, what had started off as a calamity for Nissan with the early demise of Kenny Acheson was fast turning into a disaster. Not even Steve Millen setting a new lap record of 3m40.13s on his first ever visit to La Sarthe could deflect the disappointment. And although that car would finally make it upto seventeenth, for the NISMO machine there were to be more dramas still to come, the much dreaded gearbox difficulties entering their life in the final couple of hours thereby not allowing the Japanese crew to better fifth place by flag fall. "Waddya expect from lousy Datsuns?" asked a member of The Purple Army, not waiting for or needing a reply.

Fifth and fastest lap; many teams would have been happy with that. Not so Nissan. While a banner waved defiantly by some Jaguar fans saying 'Now It Is Fall On Your Sword Time' might have been somewhat excessive and premature, no doubt back in Tokyo they were looking for those who had failed in their promises to win The Great Race to do the honourable thing. Or else.

Not that the demise of the House of Nissan left Jaguar home and dry. Quite the contrary. To avoid a recurrence of the problems encountered at Daytona earlier in the year, and bearing in mind the fate which had already befallen two of their number, as the sun grew ever hotter TWR unleashed their master plan: a bucket of water. In fact it was several buckets of water. Every time a Jaguar stopped thereafter the nose radiator would be blown out with an air jet to clear any debris which had accumulated then the whole area sluiced down with low-tech H2O.

"Waddya expect from lousy Datsuns?"

There was also the matter of some Porsches to dispose of. Contrary to most expectations the Repsol car was *still* going strong, the only hiccup to its progress being five minutes lost when it failed to restart after a pit stop, a new

battery needed before the Porsche could be sent on its way again. Nonetheless, with under six hours left it was only two laps behind the Cobb/Nielsen/Brundle car and looking ominously strong. This fact was all the more amazing because Larrauri had not yet taken part in the second part of the race having been overcome with nausea and sickness during the night. His sole contribution to the final twelve hours would be a single session beginning just after midday. The cause of his discomfort was generally regarded to be delayed shock and reaction to the unfortunate episode on Saturday morning.

One could only speculate as to how much closer the 962 would have been to the XJR12LM if 'Popi' had been available to undertake a full quota yet, in fact, on the surface of things, you hardly noticed his absence. Spurred on by some unseen guiding force Pareja and Brun were driving out of their skins, putting on the best performance of their respective careers. Even the supposed experts commentating on television were fooled, giving Larrauri credit where it was not due, Jesus and 'Walti' riding their luck and hoping for a miracle.

Joest #7 was also in with a chance. Having started so poorly, although its brakes were not all they should be the super star team of Derek Bell, Han-Joachim Stuck and Frank Jelinski were now in with more than a glimmer of hope, up to fourth, fighting Konrad/Lammers/Wallace for third and only five laps off top slot. A deficit equal to less than twenty minutes of track time, it would not take much a very serious delay on behalf of the leading XJR to put 'Dinger' in line for his sixth success, Hans his third and Frank a deserved maiden victory. Required to use Michelins rather than Goodyears did not seem to help.

And there was still the Alpha car to think about. Sixth, two laps behind the Joest Porsche and due to pick up a place with the NISMO's gearbox woes, although it would take quite a turn of events to make the magnificent black beauty into a winner stranger things have often happened.

Round and round they went, dirty and damaged, battle scarred and weary. Jaguars were being chased by Porsches who were being chased by everyone else, the distances between them all ebbing and flowing with the tide of good fortune, the positions of the top four remaining relatively static as nobody seemed willing to twist-or-bust. They knew that after so long their best chance lay not with any heroics but those ahead hitting trouble of their own. No longer were they looking for the knock out punch; now they sought to win on points.

The race was not so much quiet as careful and it was not until just before noon that things changed markedly for any of the top quartet. Joest #7 lost four laps having a broken turbo replaced, dropping it away from the Konrad/Lammers/Wallace XJR and with it any last realistic hope of victory.

Fourth would be its reward for a lot of spirited effort, the Dickens/'Winter'/Wollek sister car eighth. Suffering similar tyre and brake problems to its team leader, without a tail crunching breakfast time spin by 'Brilliant Bob' it would almost certainly finished as top 'works' car. There again, without Wollek's prowess behind the wheel it would probably have been down around fourteenth as per the third Joest 962 of Laffite/Pescarolo/Ricci. Asked later why the performance of their two 'works' cars had not been better, one Joest engineer simply shrugged his shoulders and said 'They have our tyres and we have theirs'. It was a moot point.

At about the same time as Derek Bell suffered that final ignomony in his Porsche, the C2 class was also being resolved. The engine of the Chamberlain Spice lost its oil pressure while catching the PC example, thereby leaving the Greenwich team in an unassailable position. Graff would therefore inherit second in class, thirteen laps down, Mako third, GPM fourth. Last yet not least would come the Fenwick Tiga, battling back from all manner of adversities with typical Le Mans spirit. Mazda #203 claimed the GTP category as sole survivor of the class. Curiously it was the older of their three cars, the newer two examples having broken in the night.

Porsche 'works' engineer Peter Falk looks despondent as for the third successive year defeat stares Weissach squarely in the face.

Richard Piper's Spice C2 overcame all manner of dramas to take class honours, twenty-first overall.

With the 'Lammers' XJR now relatively safe it third, all that stood between Jaguar and a Daytona type one-two was that confounded Repsol machine, the Brunmobile pulling back to within a lap of the leader when six minutes were lost by #3 having the right front caliper replaced. All race long the brakes had been poor – witness Cobb's little moment the previous evening – but the drivers had learned to live with them. Now it was a matter of nursing them to the finish.

These were tense times at Maison Jag but unless Car #3 hit more problems everyone knew, or thought they did, that there was no way the Porsche was going to catch the XJR in the time remaining. Likewise, three laps further in arrears, the second of the Jags was gradually resigning itself to third, Jan Lammers at the wheel for the final stint.

The Purple Army hadn't. While the mood in the TWR pits remained subdued, there not being much in the way of idle chit-chat or repartee, over on the terraces they were getting into their stride. Every time either of the two remaining Jaguars hurtled out of the Virage Ford and swept past them it was greeted with an energetic display of banner waving accompanied by enough cheering to keep a soccer team happy. If races were won on the terraces then this would have been a forgone conclusion long before the end. They were willing their favourites to victory, hopefully second place as well. Fortunately, nobody on the outside knew about the leaders' secret little problem. If they had done, their anticipation would have been more like anxiety.

At around about 10H30/11H00 fourth gear had failed to function, thereby requiring the drivers to short shift and be extra careful not to put too much strain on the rest of the transmission. One missed gearchange, one buzzed engine by a desperately tired driver, and what they had come so far to achieve could all be lost in a split second. No wonder the small talk was minimal.

While the Takefuji Porsche could not better twelfth, fate had an even worse result in store for the hard charging Repsol example. Pareja climbs aboard for the final stint.

LARRAURI
PAREJA
BRUN
BRUN
SPORTCARS
KENWOOD
16
¡HOLA!
SACHS
Hella
KENWOOD
OKOHAMA

Half hidden at his desk in the dugout, Tony Dowe was looking worried, his tinted spectacles hiding tired eyes which would otherwise have shown so much. He had masterminded the Daytona victory five months before and now was on the brink of an even greater success. If Jaguar #3 could hold out for a little while longer he would not only have the satisfaction of beating IMSA arch-rivals Nissan but also the 'British' TWR too. That indeed would be a victory to savour. As the race entered its final sixty minutes only the cruellest of fates would deny him such an honour.

A few minutes ago John Neilsen had climbed aboard, taking over from Martin Brundle for the run to the flag, an epic double stint in the night having more than exacted its toll on an exhausted Price Cobb. As the race wound down to the wire the moustachied American could be seen pacing pitlane, the clock now seeming to go slower than ever before. It is the waiting which is the worst part.

He was not alone. By now the immediate area had become a focus of almost all attention, media types mixing with dignitaries and team members awaiting the final outcome. Crew chief Dave Benbow, his face as impassive as ever, listened on his head-set for any inkling of trouble, fearing what he might hear. Engine wizard Allan Scott did likewise, both knowing that whatever it was it would be too late now, the Brun car away and gone by the time they had a chance to rectify any fault, however minor it may be. Close by, Tom Walkinshaw busied himself filling those oh-so-important water buckets by

way of a huge plastic can. Whatever you might think of him, there is no denying the commitment the Scot gives to his team, his hands-on approach an object lesson for all.

And now it was starting to rain! If the fickle finger of fate was going to be cruel it was certainly going about it in the wickedest of ways. TWR rolled out their wet tyres and waited for the seemingly inevitable, hoping above hope that the sudden change in conditions would not catch out either of their men, especially the one with the dicky gearbox and funny brakes.

. . . the Jaguars were nose-to-tail, the crowd going wild in double delight.

Should they bring them in? Should they keep them out? As the rain beat down harder the questions mounted. Some parts of the track were wet, others dry, you pays your money and takes your choice. Jaguar elected to stay out. It was the right choice. Twenty minutes after it started the shower passed over, a breeze coming up to hurry the dark clouds on their way.

Tiff Needell/Andrew Reid/ David Sears came home third, a virtually untroubled run paying terrific dividends for the all-British trio.

Washing your car on a Sunday is a very British tradition. Tom Walkinshaw does his thing.

A final test for TWR, one they had come through with flying colours, with half an hour to go the Jaguars were nose-to-tail, the crowd going wild with double delight. Then it was twenty-five minutes, then twenty. Time for a quick splash'n'dash.

Peeling off as if as one, down the pit road they came, John leading Jan into their respective bays. For one last time the crews went through the motions, tyres being changed in regular good order, the fuel top up completed without a hitch. Cobb gave a thumbs-up to Nielsen, Benbow the sign to go, the Dane put the XJR in gear and headed out towards the history books.

All he way up pitlane Lammers shadowed him, the oppressively large crowd hardly seeming to leave room for their safe passage. Once clear, Nielsen floored the throttle, made his way up through what remained of his gearbox, around the Dunlop Corner and away. With nothing else that he could now do to help them on their way, at last Tony Dowe climbed out of from behind his desk and into the glare of pitlane, to await the outcome. Amongst the first to offer him congratulations for what was now all but inevitable was Don Devendorf. Win and lose, they were a credit to sports car racing and IMSA in particular, as were their teams.

All around the circuit the celebrations were beginning to really take effect, the passing of the pair as if followed by a bow wave of bonhommie. The crowd were going wild, their banners waved to a crescendo, their songs starting to rise above the noise of the cars. Perhaps not quite having the special magic of 1988, nevertheless it was a wonderful thing to behold.

The last pitstop for the winners. Nielsen stays aboard for the final stint as the mechanics go about their chores for one final time.

Jaguar #2 lost out by four laps, Franz Konrad's early morning incident forever the distance between victory and first loser.

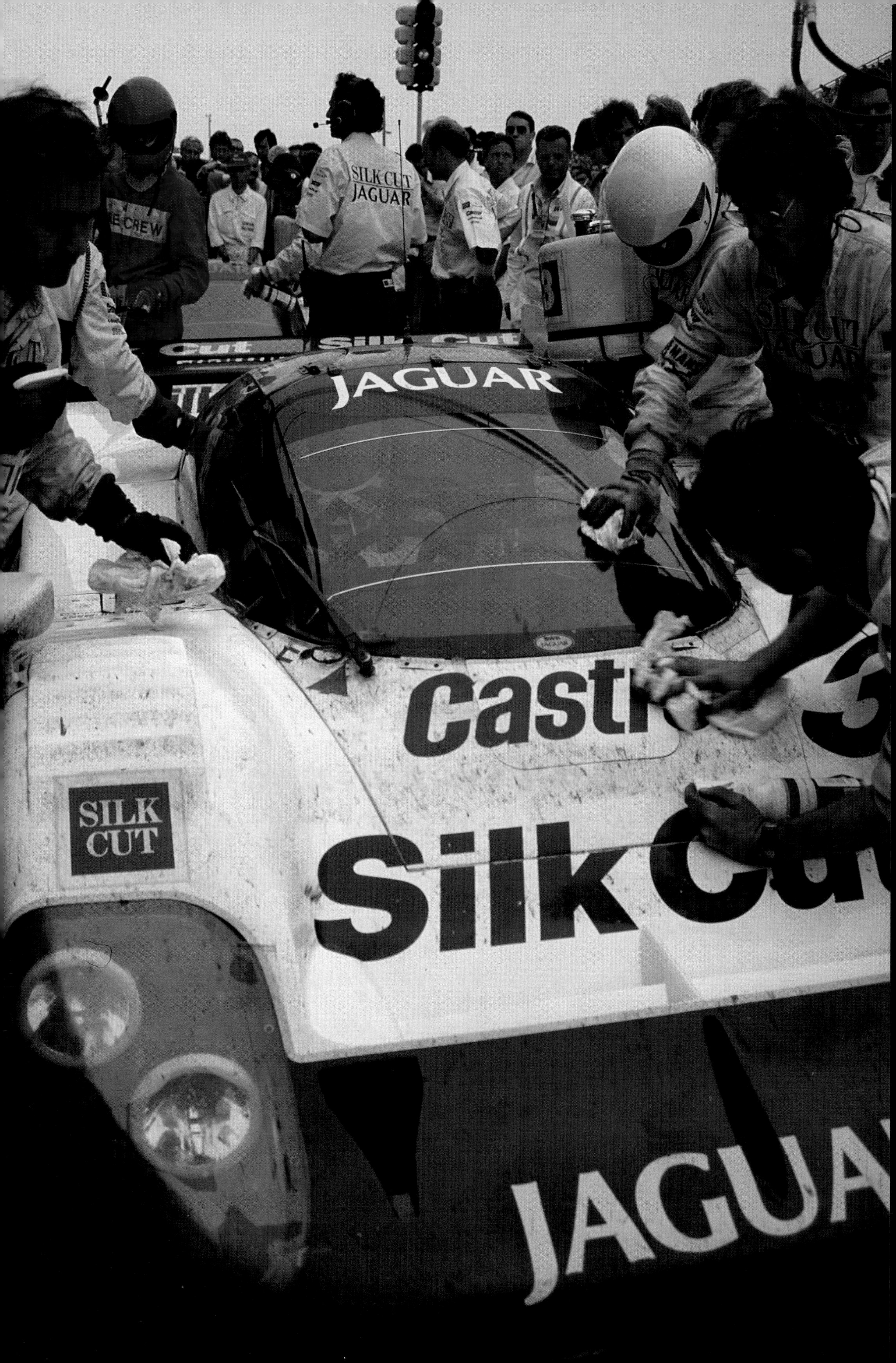
SILK CUT
JAGUAR
JAGUAR
SILK
CUT

*Nissan #23 upheld Japanese honour
with fifth overall, edging out rivals
Toyota by a lap.*

Out of sight yet not out of mind, the main contingents of the Purple Army camped opposite the pits could follow the progress of their heroes on the huge 'Diamond Vision' screen situated down by the Ford Chicane and visible nigh on the whole length of the main straight. Not surprisingly the scene the television director continued to show was of the first and third placed cars in tandem, as they had been when 'having fun' in qualifying, the clock now showing only fifteen more minutes still to run.

Suddenly the picture switched. Now it showed the run down to Mulsanne Corner and a Porsche in trouble, the Repsol 962. There, before everyones eyes, was the Brun car which had run so well for so long, its rear end wreathed in smoke and oil, crawling. Aboard it, Pareja was in agony. Not that he was physically hurt; the pain went deeper than that.

As the television screen continued to monitor its death throes the Porsche glided around the right hander and came to a stop by the signalling station. A few seconds later, as white coated marshalls decended on the stricken beast, Jesus pushed open the door, pulled himself out and without looking back walked away. Reaching his own signalling crew,

with tears rolling down his face the distraught Spaniard just put his arms on the waist- high concrete wall and lowered his head. It was an awful long way to come for nothing, a terrible end to one of the bravest and greatest races seen thereabouts for many a long day. He was inconsolable.

As were those of the team watching it all from pitlane. Nobody would have denied Brun Motorsport that second place, least of all Jaguar. Even amidst the rejoicing over their good fortune there was much commiserating with the luckless Swiss team. This wasn't business, this was sport. The only small consolation for Brun was that the demise of Repsol #16 allowed their Hydro Aluminium car into the top ten. It was like losing ten quid and finding sixpence.

The fact of the matter was that a split pipeline had cost Brun dear yet was about to give TWR a result it could not have imagined even a few short moments ago. One – two, just like at Daytona. Nobody could have asked for more.

Behind them the Minolta Toyota was grateful to have made it as high as sixth, one lap clear of the Fabre/Robert/Trolle Cougar, yet disappointed not to be able

to make up the one more lap which separated it from the NISMO Nissan and the honour of being the top Japanese car home. Next year, they vowed, next year. And one year their time will surely come.

With the demise of the Repsol car, into third slipped the Alpha 962 with its all-British driving crew, Tiff Needell proving an excellent anchor for David Sears and new boy Anthony Reid. With 'old boy' Derek Bell finishing his twentieth Le Mans in fourth it completed a great day for dear Old Blighty.

Yet the day, the weekend, the race, belonged to the victors. Denied a chance of crossing the Start/Finish Line by the invading hordes, as the crews of the first two cars assembled on the balcony to accept the congratulations of the crowd they were met with a thunderous ovation. Joined by out-going Jaguar chairman Sir John Egan – what a way to go! – and TWR boss Tom Walkinshaw it was a time for dancing and a time for singing.

"Rule Brittania, Brittania Rules Le Mans. . . ."

One-two-three-four; with one more lap
to go the crowd were already
celebrating in style.

"Go For It Lads" exclaimed the flag.
They did.

ROBIN DONOVAN (SPICE #128) : "We worked out that we would pass the leaders at about 12.15 but they stepped up their pace. We were consistently ten seconds a lap quicker than they were so reworked it out that we would get them at 2.30. Then the car blew out all its water and that was that. There probably won't be any C2 here next year so that is probably the nearest I will ever get to winning at Le Mans. End of story."

WALTER BRUN (PORSCHE #16) : "Sob, sob".

CHIP ROBINSON (NISSAN #83) : "I was really encouraged by the way we ran this year and am already looking forward to going back next year. Hopefully with an even stronger effort.

"I was really proud of the way all the IMSA people performed, not just us but all of them representing the American series. We led, we ran quick, we won via the Jag guys. It showed the competitiveness of IMSA. We may not have the strength in depth of Group C but up front it is as good."

TONY DOWE (JAGUAR TEAM) : "It is a tough race and has got much tougher. Previously Daytona was the hardest race but now I think Le Mans is, the chicanes putting a lot more load and strain on the car and personnel. It was just like being at Sebring and John Nielsen said to me that he was very confident of the car because he knew it could take that for twelve hours so he was confident of Le Mans.

"We will be using the twelve cylinder cars at Daytona again next year. . . ."

SUPER JOHN

"In America, the Nissans only usually last about eighteen hours but this is Group C, it's different. Of course, they were the biggest competition, we knew that from the beginning, but we had our set pace and decided to do that for about eighteen hours then look where we were. By that time there were no Nissans any more."

John Nielsen was not being 'bolshy', only buoyant. Renowned as one of the pleasantest people in international motor sport, after all he had good reason to be. The man they call 'Super John' had just won the world's most famous motor race.

"That's the way it goes. It's difficult. Cars break but ours kept going."

There is a world of difference between the hullabaloo of Le Mans and the peaceful tranquility of Varde, a small town on the west coast of Denmark just north of the ferry port of Esbjerg, where John Nielsen was born in 1956.

He got into motor sport by the familiar route of karts then Formula Ford, winning the Danish title in 1975 before moving on up into F.3. Although proving quick a distinct lack of finance hampered his efforts so a switch to the more lucrative European Super Vee series proved inspired, Nielsen taking the title for three consecutive years. Returning to F.3. thereafter with assistance from Volkswagen, he won the 1982 German F.3. series and looked well placed to capture the European Championship the following season only to have it snatched from his grasp by Pierluigi Martini at the last race.

Added to his disappointment there was also the embarrassment of crashing a Renault turbo F.1. car while demonstrating it at his home track of Jyllandsring, although even that paled into insignificance with a monster shunt during the 1984 Monaco F.3. race. A broken pelvis and two smashed ribs put him in hospital for five weeks and out of action for three months. Everyone thought it was the end of his career. Everyone except John.

Winning his first race back, the year ended in fine style with victory in the prestigeous Macau Grand Prix, beating off stern challenges from the likes of Stefan Johansson and Mike Thackwell in a talent filled grid. It was the perfect comeback.

Two seasons in the new F.3000 followed with a brace of wins but as his dreams of life in the Grand Prix pitlanes receded John discovered sportscars, making his Group C debut in the first

Sauber Mercedes at Le Mans in 1985. Soon he found himself cresting the hump just after the Mulsanne Kink at a full 200 mph. That is when the aerodynamic undertray broke free.

"I was just sitting there, steering, when the thing suddenly took off like an aeroplane and I realised I was flying. I thought to myself 'something has happened, there must be a big bang now'. It took a long time to hit the ground that first time and, luckily, it landed on its wheels."

What he had actually done is completed a backward somersault of which any self-respecting gymnast would be proud.

"It took me ten or fifteen laps to go flat over the little hill there after that, my brain saying to go flat but my foot lifting every time. It is not a problem any more. . . ."

"Suddenly, we were a bit scared."

John finally got to race in the WSPC a few months later, guesting for TWR Jaguar at Shah Alam in November, scoring a fine second place alongside Lammers and Thackwell.

Sauber offered him a contract for some races in 1986, so did TWR. John chose the former. It was a mistake. For the man who at that time wore a patch on his overalls stating 'There Is No Substitute For Victory' the Mercedes turbo car was still too new to get much by way of positive results from, Le Mans proving less of a disaster than before but still nothing noteworthy, both team cars out before midnight. When TWR offered him another chance for 1987 John jumped at it, winning at

Brands Hatch, a feat he repeated in 1988. He has been a mainstay of the Kidlington team ever since.

In both of the last two seasons he contested not only the WSPC but also the IMSA championships, flying backwards and forwards from his home near Hamburg in Germany almost every week. It was too much. Even this year, concentrating solely on the fifteen races of the American series plus Le Mans, will mean a lot of time spent in aeroplanes high over the Atlantic Ocean.

"The reason I like to race in America is simply because we have no fuel restrictions so you can really race and that is what I like about it. Pitstops are as quick as you can get the fuel in and tyres on, the drivers changed. There are no fuel flow limits. So it is more exciting because to me driving a race car is driving them as quick as possible, not on a computer. But next year the rules change in Group C so I might be back."

Racing in America has brought him two victories thus far, one in that much heralded 1988 Daytona 24 Hours, on TWR's IMSA debut, and again only a few weeks before Le Mans'90 at the splendidly named and located Lime Rock Park in Connecticut. There have also been more than a dozen second places in his thirty IMSA starts to date, taking him to second in the 1988 title chase, fourth last year.

As luck would have it, Lime Rock serves to amply illustrate both the good and the bad of sports car racing, U.S. style.

"The circuits are not as safe as over in Europe, most of them anyway. But you either accept what you do and do it, or you don't. There is no other alternative. I like what I do, I enjoy my job, it is both my living and my hobby. I like driving racing cars so I do it.

"Lime Rock is one of the worst, maybe not in terms of safety, but it is a rough track. It is so bumpy and old. But we had good weather, sixty-two thousand specatators and live television, so there was plenty of atmosphere. Of course we have some races which are not so good but most have an average of forty thousand spectators as well as being on tv."

For his only European outing this summer John was driving good old –288 (albeit redesignated as –1090) which is the same chassis in which he won Daytona two years ago and finished second this past February. He also finished second there in 1989, aboard – 388.

While the Daytona track has been kind to John Nielsen, not so the French classic, his two outings there with Sauber disasterous, the trio with Jaguar disappointing. On all of the last three occasions the cars had broken down late on Sunday morning after the hard work seemed to have been done. Talking only a few minutes before the start of this year's event his pre-race comments showed that he felt confident that this time it would be different. It also confirmed that instead of the new chicanes removing a danger point all they had managed to do was move it somewhere else.

"Practice went quite well, we were working on the car set-up all the way though and I think we have got a got one which will win the race for us.

"We are running a car with a lot more downforce than last year so although the straight is now slow the other corners are much quicker, especially the Porsche Curves which we now enter in fifth gear. It was quick before but now it's *really* quick!

"I am driving the 'American car'. I have done Daytona three times and finished three times with one win and two seconds. So I am confident this time is my time. We'll see."

Twenty-four hours and some minutes afterwards, in the aftermath of the post-race Press Conference there was no doubting that the event had exacted a massive physical and mental toll on the iron man from Denmark who had done virtually thirteen hours of the driving. He looked and felt exhausted.

"This was probably the hardest race ever, especially with the new chicanes. It was a a whole new ball game. The brakes were a totally unknown factor and it is something we have to work on for the future because they took a lot of punishment."

"We ran from about ten o'clock without fourth gear which was a little bit difficult because we were still under pressure from two cars (the 'Larrauri' and 'Stuck' 962s). But we figured out that even if we lost a few seconds every lap we could still win the race.

"Then, at about one/one-thirty in the afternoon, a brake caliper broke and we had to change it. It was the seals. We lost a lap on that. Suddenly we were a bit scared.

"Before the race started we talked about how unlucky I was here but we also talked about running the 'American' car. This was the first time at Le Mans in my Daytona chassis and there you go. I am not superstitious but. . . ."

Neilsen; Neilssen; Nielssen; Nilsson Schmilsson; throughout his career John Nielsen has been dogged with people spelling his name incorrectly. Even the super slick TWR Jaguar team who know how to dot an 'i' and cross a 't' often getting it wrong. On the car; in the press packs; on his overalls; there has been every spelling under the sun. But call him what you will, there is no doubt about it that Mister Nielsen is a winner.

And that's why they call him 'Super John'.

Under cover of darkness, John Nielsen gives Tom Walkinshaw a lesson in how to hold a stein of Carlsberg lager. . . .

THE PRICE OF FAME

Price Cobb and friends.

I f ever there was a man destined to do well in sports cars then it has to be Price Cobb.

In an amazing record which surely is unmatched by anybody in any type of big league motor sports anywhere in the world, he has finished in sixty-two of his sixty-six IMSA GTP starts since debuting in the series back in 1984. That's 94%!

And bearing in mind that of the unfortunate four, three of his failures have been due to engine problems and the other when his co-driver put the car off the road, there is no doubt that when it comes to getting across the finishing line the Texan who now makes his home in Colorado knows what it takes, his personal motto surely being the age old adage whereby to finish first then first you must finish.

He is good at doing that too, notching up his twelfth victory in America's premier sports car series at Lime Rock only three weeks before going to Le Mans. As is often the case these days, his partner in the Jaguar XJR10 was John Nielsen.

"The secret, if there is one, is believing in the team you are in and that you will finish the race. John and I carry that into the team, whatever. When I get into the car I just 'know' it will be there at the end. Taking care of your equipment helps but I don't think about that, its just a natural thing."

Ask any mechanic how to differentiate between someone who is kind to the equipment and someone who abuses it and he will soon point you in the direction of the gearbox engineers, the internal components of a racing transmission a foolproof guide to sorting the good from the bad. When pressed as to whether or not he is a 'softie' Mister Cobb is modest in his response.

"The gearbox guys tell us that I may or may not be, they tell us that myself and John are easier on the equipment than some others. I don't consciously make an effort to do that, it just happens. Maybe years ago when I was doing my own work I did but now I don't do that any more I don't think about it."

Thirty-five years old, those days began not with watching home grown Texas heroes such as A.J.Foyt or even Chaparral. Although he had previously played around with motorbikes and karts, his real interest in motor racing did not begin until the age of twelve when the Cobb family were living in Spain and he went to a Formula Three race at Barcelona. Amongst the drivers of the one-litre 'screamers' back then were present day sports car aces Henri Pescarolo and Derek Bell, winners of nine Le Mans races between them. Watching through the fencing of Montjuich Park on that warm spring afternoon, little did he know that he would one day get to beat them on what both had come to consider their own happy hunting ground at La Sarthe.

Like all good parents – Cobb is one of six children – they wanted their son to go to college. Price wanted to go racing. Completing a course at the famous Bob Bondurant Driving School at the now defunct Ontario Speedway in California, he started in Formula Ford in 1974 and from there soon progressed into Formula Atlantic while working for Doug Shierson, for whom Arie Luyendyk recently won the 1990 Indianapolis 500.

Shierson offered the him some Formula Atlantic outings in return for work as a mechanic on his CART team, Cobb repaying his boss' faith by coming second in the IMSA FA championship that year to Gilles Villeneuve. The following season he took it upon himself to run his own team with the same result, Villeneuve again taking the title after the Texan had engine problems in the very last round. Besides the mercurial Quebecois, competition in those days features such future stars as Danny Sullivan, Bobby Rahal and Keke Rosberg.

After that things started to fall apart, the success drying up along with the money, until he decided to quit. For two years Price Cobb was out of racing and working as a fabricator in a place which serviced turbochargers in his hometown of Dallas. Talking about it recently, the frustration of knowing he had the talent but only needed the wherewithal to prove himself is still evident in his voice. It is a story told a thousand-fold right across the full spectrum of the sport.

Then he met someone who had the money to go racing but not the know-how and despite those two wasted years Cobb soon showed that he could still do the job and took four victories en route to runner-up in the SCCA Super Vee series. But again fate dealt him a dud hand, the following year going nowhere. He went back to work as a fabricator, this time for the VDS Can-Am team. This time it really did look all over.

Then, as in all the best stories, the telephone rang. It was Rob Dyson. The two of them had first met on the Bondurant course twelve years earlier and kept in touch. While Price had tried single-seaters, Rob had gone sedan car racing when his busy schedule as a self-made man owning a number of radio stations allowed. Now he wanted to enter a Porsche 962 in IMSA GTP. What is more, he wanted Price Cobb to drive it.

His first acquaintance with the Porsche was, to quote Price's own words 'terrifying'. With its full-house ground

effects and turbocharger it was without doubt the most powerful car he had ever driven and he was not at all pleased with his performance even though he and Drake Olsen took sixth place in it at Watkins Glen. Being honest not only with himself but his friend, he told Dyson that perhaps he was not cut out for such things after all but Rob insisted he have another go at the Columbus street race in Ohio the following week.

They won. In a race of changing fortunes they used the traffic well to beat the similar car of Bob Wollek and Mauro Baldi by eight seconds, Olsen taking fastest lap and the flag.

The rest, as they say, is history. With his confidence restored and with ever growing experience in a formula he would come to almost call his own, Price Cobb logged half a dozen victories in the next two seasons, finishing as runner-up in the points chase on both occasions. He could well have won the 1987 crown from Chip Robinson if Johnny Dumfries had not thrown the car into the wall while co-driving him at the San Antonio event in Texas. Earlier in the race Price had set fastest lap.

"Needless to say, I am super happy."

Twelve months later, poetic justice saw sweet revenge as he romped home to his second win of the 1988 season there in the shadow of The Alamo. It helped secure third place in the title chase that time, behind Geoff Brabham and John Nielsen. It was also be his last for Dyson.

Mentor and friend, Rob had been with him when he had gone to Le Mans for the first time, in 1986. Sharing on of Richard Lloyd's Porsches with Mauro Baldi the trio had come ninth. He was also back in the team a year later although that was not the way it was supposed to be. Originally he had been drafted into one of the 'works' Porsches but a huge accident after hitting some freshly laid oil at the Porsche Curves early on Wednesday evening left Cobb unscathed but the car unrepairable. So he transferred along to Lloyd only to have a fire engulf that car at just around midnight when handily placed.

Twelve months later, came the offer he could not refuse. Although still an avid Porsche man, TWR USA racing chief Tony Dowe offered Price Cobb a shot at the French classic in a XJR9, something he readily accepted. Driving the 'American' car with Davy Jones and Danny Sullivan, gearbox problems eventually saw them slip to sixteenth after a strong early showing. Last year, the engine took umbrage and quit after fourteen fours.

By then Price Cobb was a fully fledged member of the TWR Jaguar line-up. Three times the winner of the prestigeous Porsche Cup, the man who had long since earned the nickname of 'Mister Consistency' had agreed to race full-time for the Coventry Cats rather than against them, Tony Dowe having offered him a season long deal in the Castrol Jaguars for 1989. Almost as a going away present to Porsche he helped Klaus Ludwig to second place in the factory managed Omron 962 at Fuji in October.

Beginning with second place for the red, white and green in the Daytona 24 Hours, it took until Portland at the end of July for Price to score a win for his new team, that being the controversial time the flag came down too early while he was engaged in earnest contest with a Nissan. After much furore, IMSA announced the final positions to be those at the time the chequered flag fell and with it Price Cobb and Jan Lammers entered the history books as the first people ever to win a major race with a turbo powered Jaguar.

A couple of months later, driving solo, he became the last of the current top breed to notch a victory in anything other than a marathon with the ubiquitous V12 by holding off the concerted effort of a Chevy Spice in the closing stages of the Tampa Challenge, the margin of victory less than three-tenth of a second after 117 fraught laps. Again it helped him to third in the final standings, that first championship still tantalisingly close but also as far away as ever.

He needs look no further for similar success au Sarthe. During the course of the week, and soon after the race had been won, he had spoken of the track, the car, and what it was like to win the World's most famous motor race. Almost inevitably the conversations began with the new chicanes.

"Coming into this race I was a little bit concerned that the Mulsanne was no longer there for our cars' strength, the

V12 Jaguars having always been incredibly quick down there and I was worried that a turbo car can come off the corners quicker now that they've added two on that long straightaway, taking away our advantage. Or so we thought.

"We also thought that it would affect our fuel mileage greatly. As it turned out, what with the new Goodyear tyres on our car and the fact that we ran a bit more downforce, the car was very well balanced, allowing us to keep within the fuel mileage regulations, and pursue a great pace.

"Based on our performance at Daytona these past few years we decided to set not a blistering pace but a strong one, hoping that everyone else would follow. If we needed to adjust it we could have done so accordingly. If someone had gone off at a rabbits pace, one or two seconds a lap faster than us, we were certainly not going to let that bother us until a long way down the road. As it turned out we did set the pace and we were the ones that people followed."

Not that life was not without its complications. Firstly there was the fact that (as with Daytona this year) he had not done much work in the latter stages of the race, leaving it to his partners to bring home the victory.

"I have always had a bit of a heat problem. Once I get too hot I am finished but these two guys carried the day. The entire team has been outstanding. To see the work that goes on from both sides of 'The Pond' and see the whole thing come together is a real pleasure."

There was also the not inconsiderable matter of the brake problem only a few hours from the finish, Jaguar #3 losing one of its two laps advantage over all pursuers as the pit crew went about replacing a leaking caliper.

"I was heartbroken. It was a routine brake pad stop and when they went to replace the pads they noticed a leak and you certainly can't ignore it. They did a phenomenal job on that right front corner which kept us at least one lap ahead and the two of them then nursed the car right to the end, keeping the pressure on the Repsol Porsche and that gave us the win."

But all is well that ends well and in the end Price Cobb was there to cheer his team mates home, those dark days long ago when he despaired of ever getting his racing career together all but forgotten in the euphoria.

"Needless to say, I am super happy. I was originally hired to race for the Castrol Jaguar team in the USA and this is beyond my wildest dreams. Certainly, without John and Martin it would not have happened."

Not that the success was likely to phase someone who had come up the hard way, taken the knocks and got to the top.

"I will enjoy it until the next race. Then it's back to square one."

And just to make sure that this charming man who is pursuing his pilot's licence keeps his feet firmly on the ground, when he got back home to Colorado after the race he was greeted with the news that the youngest of his two daughters was suffering from chicken pox.

Welcome home, Daddy! Welcome home, Le Mans winner!

GRASS ROOTS RACER

It is a long way to the victory rostrum at Le Mans from the grass tracks of Norfolk where Martin Brundle first started racing as a thirteen years old back in 1972, firstly with a Ford Anglia then a Hillman Minx. After that it was a spell in hot rods.

In 1977 he then transferred his attentions to 'proper' motor racing, contesting the British Saloon Car Championship in a Toyota Celica. In his very first race he took pole position but spun out following tyre failure.

Over the next few years Martin then mixed saloons with single seaters, the most notable episodes being the winning of the 1980 BMW County Championship, a one-make series whose cars were prepared by TWR, then being recruited as team mate to an un-retired Stirling Moss in the BSCC Audis the following season. Two years later he only lost the 1983 British Formula Three Championship to Ayrton Senna at the very last round following some epic and memorable dices.

1983 also saw the beginning of his long association with Tom Walkinshaw's Jaguars, winning in an TWR XJS at both Donington and Zeltweg. The following season won at Enna-Pergusa.

But by then he had also been signed up by the greatest talent spotter of them all, Ken Tyrrell, and was in Formula One, scoring a marvellous fifth place with two points on his Grand Prix debut in Brazil. A few months later a superb second place at Detroit confirmed his arrival in the top echelon only for the world to fall in around him when Team Tyrrell were disqualified (due to supposed fuel irregularities) from the race and erased from the series, the official Longines/Olivetti directory not even acknowledging the team having been present at all that year. One can only speculate that injuries Martin subsequently received in an accident at Dallas before the ban was confirmed must have been imaginary. The pain wasn't.

Staying with the Ockham marque another two seasons, scoring points on four occasions, Brundle then joined Zakspeed. That proved to be a downwards step and after only one season he announced his withdrawal from F.1. to concentrate on sports cars for 1988.

He had been involved with TWR and its World Sport-Prototype Championship racing programme since the inception, even taking the lead on its debut at Mosport Park in August of 1985 for a few glorious laps. Switching cars after

the first one failed, he then netted third at the end. Unfortunately, outings for the Kidlingtom marque were few and far between thereafter, especially when Tyrrell placed an embargo on extra-cirricular activities following the death of Stefan Bellof. Nonetheless, he had helped Raul Boesel to the 1987 crown by winning at Spa.

Now it was his turn, taking the 1988 World Sports-Prototype Championship for Drivers with victories at Jarama, Monza, Silverstone, Brands Hatch and Fuji.

In between, he was also a major figure in TWR's initial foray into IMSA, taking well deserved wins in the Daytona 24 Hours at the first attempt and the lucrative Del Mar 'Money Race' to crown a fine season.

Having completed most of what he set out to – the IMSA title would have been a bonus – Brundle reverted to F.1. with Brabham for 1989, soon realising the error of his ways. Shortly before the current season opened he again announced his withdrawal from Grands Prix and joined TWR full time. He had taken part in sixty-nine G.P.s including those seven 'non-existant' ones.

Second place first time out, at Daytona, he later netted an excellent victory at Silverstone. Then came Le Mans.

Speaking at the end of a great week, King's Lynn's favourite son had this to say:

"Tom Walkinshaw had a strategy for the whole race and it all turned out exactly as planned so we were probably a little bit more under control that what it might have looked like at the time. Yes, I did set out to try and win it in Car #1 but the whole strategy was to push the opposition as hard as we could with two of our cars and keep the other two for the end of the race. That worked out absolutely perfectly, even the right numbers doing the right jobs.

"I have driven with John Nielsen in a lot of 24 Hours races. We did the first Daytona together, which we won, and have always come close to repeating it here at Le Mans. So to actually do it with John, and Price Cobb, is obviously very special because we were so disappointed at Daytona this year when we finished second, albeit to our sister car.

"This was a team effort. The whole TWR Silk Cut Jaguar effort is not just down to a few people, it is a hundred plus people here plus all those back at base building the cars. It was a six months programme and, remember, we are not running the cars here that we race in the sprint championship so TWR have done all of this Le Mans in amongst doing the sprint turbo car for the World Championship, which is quite phenomenal."

INDIANA BRIT

While it is the drivers and the team owner who usually get all the credit for a race win, especially the big ones, behind them are a loyal and dedicated team of engineers. This year much was made of the fact that the winning car was the 'American' Jaguar and therefore the spotlight fell squarely on Tony Dowe, the man who has masterminded all TWR USA racing efforts from its base at Valparaiso in Indiana, including both Daytona 24 Hours victories. To paraphrase Joel Grey upon receiving his Oscar for 'Cabaret', it has taken nearly twenty years of hard toil to become an overnight sensation. . . .

Born in Norfolk in 1948, Tony was educated at the Chelsea School of Aeronautical and Automobile Engineering. For a while he owned his own kart preparation company, building the engines for a number of World Cup winners.

In 1976 he entered top flight motor sport, working with Clay Regazzoni as chief mechanic on the Tissot Ensign. After that it was a spell at Brabham where the incumbent drivers included Hans-Joachim Stuck, Andreas-Nikolaus Lauda and John Marshall Watson. Amongst the innovative Gordon Murray designs back then was the legendary BT46 'fan' car. His last taste of Formula One came with James Hunt and the Wolf.

In 1979, Tony decided to seek new challenges and accepted a position as crew chief of the Newman/Freeman Can-Am team, Elliott Forbes-Robinson and Keke Rosberg then in the driving seats, before going to work for Haas Racing for whom Patrick Tambay won the 1980 SCCA Can-Am crown.

He even tried his hand at Indycars, with Johnny Rutherford in 1982/83, before settling down to become General Manager of Carl A Haas Automobile Imports. Amongst his various business interests, Haas being the main importer of Lola cars and Hewland transmissions into the USA. Tony was there four years, the longest single stay of his career thus far.

Then came the offer he could not refuse.

PARADISE LOST

Amongst the winners there are always losers. Some come close to success but fall at the final hurdle. Eliseo Salazar came closer than most.

Sitting surrounded by people yet alone in his thoughts, he was the one who missed out on the good times at Le Mans this year. Having been slotted in alongside Price Cobb and John Nielsen during qualifying, doing a competent job, TWR tactics dictated that Eliseo be kept in reserve so as to be fresh to help out wherever needed should Cobb suffer a recurrence of his Daytona heat exhaustion or any unforseen eventualities arise.

Just when he was going to get in on the act and take over behind the wheel of what would ultimately become the winning car, Jaguar #1 expired and Martin Brundle was transferred across

instead. Although the Chilean got a run in the 'Jones' XJR it was nowhere near the same, not even finishing. Unless a miracle happens Eliseo Salazar will forever be haunted by the fact that he is the Le Mans winner who never won the race.

It was his fifth attempt at the 24 Hours, the first two back in the early eighties in Dome Fords, then for Spice in 1988 and Jaguar last year. It was aboard the XJR9 that he recorded his first ever finish, eighth with the Ferte brothers.

The son of a wealthy industrialist, Eliseo was born in Santiago de Chile in 1954 and started racing sixteen years ago in a Mini Cooper. In 1978 he was the Argentinian Formula Four champion.

Inspired by such progress he then came to Britain and soon found himself in F.3., transferring to Aurora F.1. for

1980. Driving a Williams FW07, very much a state of the art Grand Prix machine at that time, he recorded seven pole positions and three victories on his way to second place in the final championship standings behind Emileo de Villota.

Continuing the upward spiral, for 1981 it was into Grands Prix. After a fraught time with a RAM-March he went to Ensign, scoring a fine sixth place in Holland. Fifth at Imola in 1982 with ATS were his only other F.1. points, his G.P. career coming to an end in mid'83 after trying to make something of the recalcitrant RAM. He had disputed twenty-four Grands Prix but, alas, will forever be most remembered in motor racing circles as the human punch bag for Nelson Piquet's disgraceful antics at Hockenheim in 1982.

Until now.

Some you win, others you lose. Eliseo Salazar managed both at the same time.

CLASSMATES

MIKE YOULES :

A regular spectator at Le Mans since 1975, Mike is one of those lucky fellows to have won his class at the first attempt.

He started racing about ten years ago and has since campaigned such diversities as a Lotus Elan, Historic F3s and Porsche RSR before turning to the BRDC sports car series in recent seasons. His 'day job' is as the owner of a company which does interior refurbishment of commercial premises. He is 34-years old.

"One of the overwhelming memories I have is that before we got on the rostrum we were in the anti-room when the Jaguar team went out and got the applause. And we thought it would have quietened down when we did but there must have been about sixty thousand people in pitroad, on the track, in the grandstands, everywhere. They gave us a fantastic reception. It was terrific of them to stay on to do so."

RICHARD PIPER :

Co-director with Patric Capon of P C Automotive, based in Greenwich, London. Richard is 42-years old and started his racing in Mini Coopers back in 1969.

Since then he has tried almost everything from Formula Ford to Historic F.1., IMSA and Thundersports. 1990 was the first time he had driven at Le Mans although he had been twice recent years as a team manager, failing to finish both times.

OLINDO IACOBELLI :

Born in 1945 and hailing from Detroit, this was Olin's third attempt to finish at Le Mans, failing to get to Sunday sunrise on each of his previous two attempts.

His wide variety of motor sports interests have included dragsters and stock cars plus some Formula Three before concentrating on sports cars.

YOSHIMI KATAYAMA :

The senior member of the Mazda team, Katayama was fifty years old one month prior to the race. Runner-up in the 1967 50cc World Motorcycle Chsampionship, his four wheeled successes include being japanese Endurance Champion of 1977 and '78 plus a Daytona 24 Hours class winner in 1979 and '82. Missed last year's race due to food poisoning. Seven appearances at Le Mans with three class wins.

YOJIRO TERADA :

A Mazdaspeed development engineer who first competed at Le Mans in 1974 with the Sygma. 1990 marked his twelfth participation and third class victory. His c.v. also includes three Daytona 24 class wins. Has an unrivalled experience of racing with rotary engines. Born in 1947.

TAKASHI YORINO :

The younger brother of Yoshimi Katayama, this was his second Le Mans class win in nine attempts. Won the 1972 Japanese Touring Car series and 1977 Japanese Endurance Championship. Also has two Daytona 24 Hours class wins to his credit. 39-years old.

Youles, Piper and Iacobelli; C2 winners.

GASOLINE ALLEY BRED

JAGUAR :

As per last year, TWR turned up with four cars. They were Car #1 – chassis 990, Car #2 – 290, Car #3 – 1090 and Car #4 – 190. The two even numbered race cars were assembled around brand new monocoques which had been delivered to Kidlington way back in January, the cars being built up with meticulous care and attention by a special in-house team over the course of the next six months. The other two, the odd numbered race cars, were built up around redesignated IMSA tubs.

Car #1, previously –388 and now – 990, had come third in the 1988 Daytona 24 Hours, second last year and won it in 1990. This was its first visit to Le Mans.

Car #3, now known as –1090, had a previous life form as –288 and as such also an interesting history. This was the vehicle which won the 1988 Daytona 24 Hours, formed the basis of the 'Lammers' car twelve months later (it did not finish) and came second this time around. As an aside, it competed at Le Mans last year, leading awhile in the hands of Davy Jones and Derek Daly before succumbing to gearbox then engine difficulties. This time things would be better. . . .

While Car #1 also came under the auspices of Kidlington, Car #3 was put together at the team's IMSA base in Indiana and as such featured a number of detail modifications based on their experience of the rough and tough washboard tracks of North America, Sebring being a classic example. It was fitted with different roll-bars and suspension geometry. All four vehicles had their 1990 spec- Group C bodywork fitted in England.

The aerodynamic package for the revised circuit, more of a guesstimate than before as nobody had been afforded any opportunity to try it out beforehand, was the work of longtime respected TWR engineer Alistair McQueen. Technically, most of the changes were in the underbody to generate more downforce with the latest shape described as being half way between the previous year's low downforce set-up and a high downforce 'sprint' version. This resulted in a benefit which one noted insider described to be 'fifty per cent more than not a lot'.

Although the circuit changes took some speed out of the long straight the increased download gave better traction at other parts of the circuit, thereby making the already notorious section from Mulsanne Corner to Indianapolis and the dreaded Porsche Curves even quicker than before!

Modellers will be interested to note that what subsequently became the winning car had one long and one short antenna rather than the two longer aerials of the others. It was also the only one not to have a roof mounted identification light and the only one whose dash-top mounted computer box was blue rather than silver. The second placed car had logos beneath the door stating 'Jaguar Holland' in support of Jan Lammers.

Jaguar #1 had its front tow-hook on the right-hand side, the others on the left. Just to complete the series off oddities, Jaguar #4 had a huge red dot on its engine cover, signifying it as the camera car for low flying helicopters.

All four were on Goodyear tyres. The XJR12LMs officially weighed in at 931, 938, 953 and 949 kilos respectively. Other than differing liquid loads, it is hard to fathom what would have made for such large discrepancies. . . .

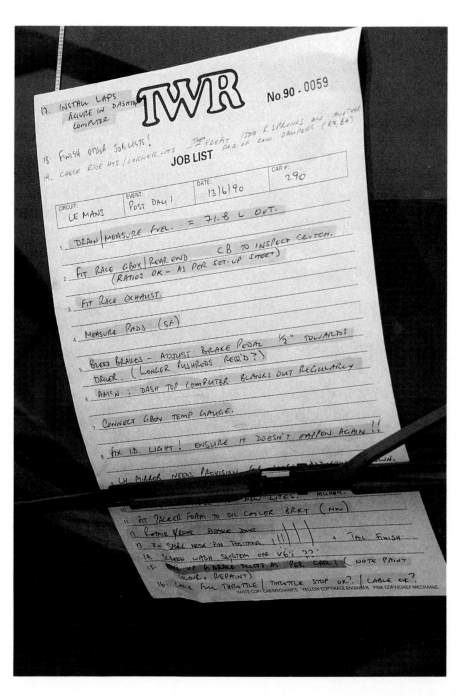

PORSCHE :

There were nineteen Porsche 962s entered, four of them by the factory favoured Joest team, although both totals were promptly reduced by one when Jonathan Palmer destroyed 962–013 early on Wednesday evening. It had, until then, been a brand new chassis.

A second new tub, 962–015, was entered for Bell/Jelinski/Stuck while the other two trios relied on a pair from last year's batch. All were in long tail/low downforce trim in readiness for the altered Mulsanne. The lead car sported a 3.2 litre engine during qualifying but reverted to a 3.0 litre for the race in keeping with the other team cars.

Brun Motorsport was a keen advocate of the short tail/high downforce set-up and also had a 3.2 litre unit for qualifying, theirs as with all the other non-factory supplied 'superunits' coming from Andial in California. Suitably armed, Larrauri used chassis –150 to set his front row time, that then promptly put away and replaced by –160 for the race itself. A third Repsol liveried car was also in attendance but not used, being brought to Le Mans (supposedly) en route to Jarama. Their Hydro Aluminium car, 003BM, incorporates a Thompson rather than a Stuttgart chassis and was last year's FromA Porsche.

Alpha was also a name on the Brunmobiles last time around but on this occasion the recently formed Tomei Engineering team was entrusted to do the honours. Using 962-154, like Brun they too were on Yokohamas with a low downforce set-up although they did experiment briefly with the alternative package early on Thursday before reverting to their race trim.

Trust Racing were another top Japanese outfit at Le Mans for the first time, chassis 962-159 having its first race too. At home they normally race a Lloyd chassised car.

Richard Lloyd was covering his options. Not only did he have one of his own creations, identified as GTi–201, with its composite and honeycomb panels, but also another brand new Stuttgart example, 962-161 being the property of pop drummer and motor racing stalwart Nick Mason. The RLR built device was in short tail trim, the factory model in long tail, it only being delivered to the team from Stuttgart a week before the race. As such it represents the last Porsche 962 to date.

Team Schuppan were also giving themselves options, using one of their own carbon composite creations in the blue Omron #55 car and Stuttgart tub 962-146 in the bright red Takefuji #33 machine. Both were in high downforce mode.

Last of the C1 Porsches were those of Tim Lee-Davey, offering us 962-138/001 and 962-138/002, both with Schuppan tubs. The real 962-138 was on a car sold to an American collector late last year. A supposed third entry was scratched.

Kremer were the third Porsche outfit wearing Yokohama rubber but had taken the factory's suggestions to heart and opted for a high downforce arrangement. They were utilising two Thompson CK6 composite chassies.

Obermaier were another two car Porsche team, the Primagaz pair boosted by Harald Groh's first day sixth best time again courtesy of a special 3.2 litre Andial unit.

One other Porsche 962 was present, the Momo/Gebhardt IMSA car with its Thompson chassis –001GS having been extensively rebuilt since Derek Bell upended it at Daytona in February.

SPICE :

The only contender in the 3.5 litre/750 kgs category once the GPM car consumed its engines and failed to make the grid, the Raika name discarded by Momo first appeared on the 'works' Spice C1 on Thursday very much as an after-thought then on Saturday in all its proper splendour. As for the machinery itself, this year's version incorporates enclosed rear wheels a' la Jaguar otherwise it was 'simply' a beefed up version of the 1989 model.

All the six C2 Spices were also Cosworth V8 powered, albeit in less highly tuned form. Graff and Lombardi were making their annual appearances, the British quartet of reigning WSPC C2 champions Chamberlain there with GPM, Mako and PC Automotive.

The most interesting technically was Chamberlain's SE89C owned by 'Charles Hausmann' and featuring C1 style brakes and revised suspension, etcetera. Mako was the prettiest.

NORMA :

Someone supposed to be challenging Spice in normally aspirated and fuel-free C1 was Norbert Santos' Norma MGN M6. Although the neat composite chassis was seen, the W12 engine was not. . . .

CANARY EAGLE :

A more glorious failure was the Canary. Without a doubt one of the most interesting cars seen at Le Mans for many years was the ex-works Lola Corvette of Paul Canary and friends, now redubbed as an Eagle although bearing nothing but the name in common with Dan Gurney's AAR Toyota Eagles of IMSA GTP fame.

The car had a choice of engines, either a 10.2 litres or a more humble 9.4 litre version, the thirty-two valve all-alloy V8s being built by Joe Schubek of Eagle Engines in California, ostensibly for drag racing. Sadly, that seems to be their niche because over the course of practice they seemed incapable of holding together for more than a quarter-mile or few seconds at a time. But it sure sounded good while it lasted!

NISSAN :

A huge effort by Nissan this year was headed by no less than seven cars, five entered by 'works' backed teams and two handed over to privateers.

NISMO, the Japanese part of the equation, ran one with two each being operated by Nissan Motorsports Europe and NPTI, the reigning double IMSA champions better known by their former independent name of Electramotive. The NISMO car was a development of ones used in the Japanese Endurance Championship and in its R90CP trim offered significantly different body styling to the rest. The other four 'works' cars were pukka WSPC Group C and designated as R90CKs. Mark Blundell used a specially prepared sixth car for his extra-hot qualifying lappery. All had the latest VRH35Z 3.5 litre turbocharged V8s, Blundell's qualifying special reckoned at well over 1000 bhp.

The two 'American' cars elected to run with steel brake discs, the other three operating with carbon components. The IMSA boys also had Goodyears while the others had to make do with Dunlops. As always NPTI was headed by Don Devendorf.

One of last year's R89Cs was to be in the care of Team Le Mans, Tom Hanewa's perenially enthusiastic visitors, while the other would be under the wing of Yves Courage and his Cougar equipe. Both were very much 'showroom stock' and unchanged from 1989.

TOYOTA :

While their Japanese rivals hogged all the pre-race headlines, Toyota were discreetly low profile. They had three cars, two operated by TOM'S and the third by SARD (the red one) for whom Keith Greene was on the payroll.

The R90-CVs came with their new six-speed gearboxes but not the 3.6 litre V8s, Toyota preferring to utilise the older 3.2 litre versions instead.

New steel brakes were fitted, replacing last year's carbon ones and the wheelbase extended slightly from 1989.

MAZDA :

Three IMSA GTP Mazdas were entered, two new 787s and a revised 767B. Dramatically different styling particularly around the back was the most obvious visual alteration, especially the half enclosed rear wheels. The radiator was now front mounted.

Equally as significant was the radically new four rotor R26B engine with its so-called telescopic intake manifold system, triple plug ignition system and peripheral port injection. Together they helped bring about better performance and greatly reduced fuel consumption for less weight.

And if all that was not enough Mazda were employing six-times winner Jacky Ickx as a consultant team manager.

COUGAR :

Besides having a Nissan to use, Cougar also turned up with two of their neat aluminium honeycomb C24S Porsche powered devices, both of which had also reverted to steel brakes after having flirted with carbon. Improved engine installation and revised intercoolers were noted.

The 1989 C2 class winning Cougar Porsche was entered under the Chereau banner yet was still a 'works' operated car, making it a very busy weekend for the local heroes.

LANCIA :

The latest recycling of 'The Italian Job' featured heavily modified suspension, revised engines and just about everything else. Fitted with a newly built chassis hardly anything of the original LC2 now survives, even less after race day!

THE OTHERS :

ADA, ALD and Argo made up the entry, plus a Tiga. With revised aerodynamics the ADA looked the part but was soon brought down to earth at scrutineering when the windscreen was declared to low. This was rectified by putting more 'gunge' underneath it! The ALD was one of the Paris team's latest composite chassies, the Argo also brand new. All three used the ubiquitous Cosworth V8 as did the Tiga which was entered under the GPM banner but otherwise independent. An ex-Roy Baker Racing GC288 it is a familiar sight on the British 'clubbie' scene.

MILD AND BITTER

Chamberlain Engineering first came to Le Mans in 1987 when Nick Adams set an excellent C2 pole in the omnipotent Spice Hart turbo, repeating the exercise twelve months later with a time which beat no less than fourteen C1 machines. There was also a second car for a trio of Frenchman. None finished.

Last year the result was the same. With one car out early, a lead of fifteen laps for the other over allcomers counted for nothing when the engine broke a valve just around breakfast time. As before, the Buntingford based team had come a long way for no reward.

This year they were determined to make it pay. If the Jarama WSPC race had been cancelled at reasonable notice rather than at the fifty-ninth minute of the eleventh hour, Hugh would have brought his two C1-spec WSPC Spice Cosworths. As it was they were being readied for what turned out to be a non-event and he instead entered the C2 SE89C owned and raced by pseudonymous Dutch businessman 'Charles Hausmann', usually in Interserie.

Yet although Chamberlain Engineering were the reigning and final WSPC C2 champions, the category being dropped from this year's series, most of the pundits dismissed their chances as negligible, especially by virtue of the fact that none of its regular drivers were in the team this time. Sponsorship and other considerations meant they had either found employment elsewhere or taken the weekend off.

Teamed with Le Mans rookie 'Hausmann' were Philippe de Henning and Robin Donovan. Baron de Henning had won the class three years ago in the factory Spice while 'Dobbin' was a veteran of four brave, albeit unrewarding, campaigns thus far. The first knew the car but not the track, the other two the track but not the car. Robin had never driven a Spice before, nor raced at all for seven months. Competent rather than quick, nobody except the team themselves really expected the Buntingford Beastie to growl, only whimper. Oh ye of little faith.

Nevertheless, not surprisingly qualifying was somewhat low key, especially on Wednesday, the drivers getting to know the car and the team and the new chicanes, the superfast times of bygone years precisely that. Not that it was easy going.

Trying to avoid exhausting everybody at once, due to the close proximity of the supposed Jarama race they had come with a skeleton crew, the rest of whom

"If they are going to throw it in the wall I want them to do it by five o'clock tomorrow evening so that I can go and have a few beers. If they are not going to do that then I want them to continue to four o'clock the next afternoon. If it is eight or nine or ten on Sunday morning I will get *very* cross. I've done that the last two years and that really does upset me!"

It was Friday lunchtime and Hugh Chamberlain was on top form. If their is anyone in sports car racing who embodies the bulldog spirit of fair play, hard graft and that motor racing is meant to be fun, it is the very amiable ex-policeman from Scotland. His abundant easy banter hides a steely determination, his quotable quotes disguise a fierce competitive edge. Hugh Chamberlain might not run the biggest or best motor racing team in the world but he was here and he was determined to win.

were due to arrive for the weekend. The car had then been allocated a late scrutineering time and never got back to the circuit until gone ten o'clock on Tuesday night. With only two mechanics available to change from the race engine (as fitted upon arrival) to the qualifying unit needed on Wednesday, it took all day rather than the three hours or so a full staff could have done it in, the job finally being completed just after the first period got under way.

This meant there was no time to change the gear ratios too, the fall-back plan to alter them during the break between the two sessions thwarted when the schedule was revised following Jonathan Palmer's accident. Having already lost time at the beginning of the early period it was decided not to jeopardise their chances by losing more. Proper ratios or not, it was better to get all of the drivers qualified just in case rain or some other unforseen problem caused havoc with their Thursday programme. It was better to be safe than sorry.

Overnight the engine was switched back again, the race unit being installed, as were the the race brakes and bodywork. The gear ratios were finally changed too. Despite being limited to 7500 rpm, this enabled Philippe to improve its best time by a couple of seconds although not its grid position, Chamberlain Spice #128 destined to start from Row23 alongside Richard Piper's PC Automotive version. Nine places up the grid class favourites Mako looked ominously strong, a whopping sixteen seconds to the good. Not that such things worried Hugh unduly.

"The drivers complained that we gave them no grip, no brakes and no gears in the right places. Even so they are seconds quicker than I told them to run. They can go quicker still but we don't want them to!

"It really was terribly boring. The drivers wanted to go out and play all the time and we were finding excuses for them not to, or having to tell them they could not. The further it went on the more annoyed they got. But basically, there was no real problem. We just did what we had to do."

With their on-track dramas restricted only to an alternator belt coming adrift on Wednesday, 'boring' might not have been the word most people used to describe qualifying for The Great Race but it was better than having a disaster on their hands. 'Hausmann' would start, followed in true Chamberlain-speak 'by one of the other two, followed by the third one'. Run in such spirit, it had all the makings of a great race.

When the green lights came on 'Charles' was soon in his stride, the statistics of the first sixty minutes showing him to be thirty-fifth, the next few hours seeing 'one of the other two' and 'the third one' staying in the overall mid-thirties.

With a quarter of the race run, the pair of French run Spices from Lombardi and Graff held a one lap advantage over the Piper PC SE89C, the Chamberlain version maintaining close contact with the ADA in their battle for fourth place five laps off the lead. A couple more further back was the Mako car, its race engine not proving to have the same healthy grunt as its qualifying unit. Acquiring a flavour for gearboxes would not help it either, three being changed during the course of events. Although John McNeil's immaculate little team would soldier on they would never figure in the C2 lead battle, thereby putting a not-so-swift end to one of Hugh's pre-race theories and speculations.

"There are two other Spice teams who could win, three if you take in the frogs. Mako, Richard Piper and Graff. Mako must be favourites. As with the Piper car it isn't used much, neither of them being in the WSPC. As for Graff, he doesn't do anything but lie in the bath dreaming of Le Mans. But we'll be there. If any of the four teams – including ourselves – has a trouble free run it'll win by best part of an hour. Or half a lap."

Already out were the ALD and C2 Cougar, the Fenwick Tiga much delayed. Nor was the GPM Spice on target, the Silverstone based team another which would battle to the end without disturbing the class leader board to any great extent.

Not that things were going entirely according to plan chez Chamberlain. There were problems with the gearbox but they did not know exactly what. The gearlever knob had also fallen off. Quite unrelated, it would prove to be an ominous sign.

There had also been the unusual difficulty of the seat breaking loose thereby requiring Robin Donovan to hang on to the steering wheel as his only means of support as he was rocked and rolled about inside the cockpit. More of a problem than it might sound, that alone accounted for most of their lost laps. Undeterred, the ever ebullient and

optimistic 'Uncle Hugh' was looking on the bright side.

"The brakes are alright, the engine is running fine. We are a bit out on fuel because the drivers are going too quickly and we cannot slow them down.

"I thought the transmission was going to be fun and is proving to be a bit of a problem but it is not the end of the world. I think we have got just about everything cracked at the moment. All we need is the four cars in front of us to blow up and we will be in real good order. Then we can have a race with the only other one left to the finish!"

He was also aware that with the dramas they had suffered so far, although minor compared to those encountered by others, there was no doubting that the Chamberlain SE89C should have been, in his own words, 'six weeks down'. As it was they were only five laps behind and still in with a chance.

He also knew that he had gone into the race with drivers who, by general consensus, were not of the same calibre as his regular crew. That is not to say they are not good drivers, they are, and they were doing superbly because it was the machinery which was letting them down, not vice-versa.

"They are behaving remarkably well" he confided in a stage whisper above the roar of the passing traffic. "It's very worrying!"

As darkness descended so the drama increased. Soon the leaders were in trouble, Graff with electrical gremlins, Lombardi a broken gearbox. They would be out of the race for over an hour apiece, the latter destined to return only to be crashed just after dawn. As a consequence, this left the Piper car out front and with the ADA plodding reliably if not rapidly on, as they approached the witching hour the Chamberlain SE89C found itself promoted to second. And closing.

And even closer when Piper lost a lap having its rear wing replaced after being clouted by a spinning Kremer Porsche at the second Mulsanne chicane shortly before midnight.

Four laps apart as Saturday night became Sunday morning, as the temperature went down so the stakes went up, the gap reduced to two laps within the next hour, the Piper/Iacobelli/Youles lead only ninety seconds by the time the next bulletin was posted. Robin Donovan put in a particularly impressive double stint at this time, his performance level being matched by 'Hausmann' and de Henning during their own periods at the wheel. Despite their troubles with the gearbox and despite themselves the Chamberlain crew were driving the race of their lives.

They took the lead just before the end of the eleventh hour. It did not last. A few minutes later, at 03H28 Philippe de Henning pulled into the pits, the gearbox finally having given up the fight. The team boss was amongst those there to greet him.

"We have had a gearbox problem since early on. We did not quite know what it was until it exploded in a heap of porridge and bits. The poor guy was left with a 'box with only second and third but he brought it home saying 'this is not very quick in a straight line, guv' so we had to start repairing it. We took the whole thing apart, taking a lot of bits and pieces out and putting a lot of bits and pieces back."

It took fifty minutes, by which time Piper & Co. were up and away. With nobody else in a position to challenge them you could almost hear the sigh of relief above the pitlane noise. Chamberlain eventually resumed in second place, ten laps down with best part of twelve hours still to go. There was nothing left to do but continue the chase.

Down came the time and down came the distance. There was no doubt about it Chamberlain were putting up a great fight, edging ever closer with each passing lap, taking ten seconds a tour off the leader.

Then came the break they needed. By 08H00 the gap was seven laps, an hour later it was only three. A broken rear rocker arm on the PC Spice had needed replacing, GPM doing the sporting thing and lending Piper a spare despite languishing at the rear of the field with their own tales of woe. It was a terrific gesture, one typical of the bonhomie of C2. From only a few pits away Hugh Chamberlain had watched the repair being undertaken with more than casual interest. He knew that as things were going he might yet pull off the big prize.

"It would be very nice if we could both go to the finish without problems then we would have a race to the flag for the first time in C2 for three hundred years. That would be good fun. We are catching them at about ten seconds a lap. If we don't have any trouble and they don't have any trouble it is physically possible that we will catch them and we will win."

Yet as he talked he knew it would not be easy. Both cars, like all the other battered and bruised projectiles still running, were decidedly the worse for wear.

"We still have something like seven hours to go and in the good old days of 1000Kms racing I would not have considered pushing a car in the state that ours is now into the car park let alone onto the grid of a race. We have an hour to go before that would start yet.

"Our clutch is in a very bad, our gearbox selecting whichever one it happens to think about at the time. But our drivers have behaved impeccably. I thought they would not have the experience between them to hold the car together, it's not the easiest thing in the world to do this damn place day and night, sunshine and showers, yet they have behaved impeccably so far – other than that they won't slow down!"

Seven hour then six. PC tried upping their pace to stabilise the gap but could not do so by much, their engine already consuming more oil than was healthy for it, a bad sign at the best of times. They led, Chamberlain followed, battle had been well and truly joined. Survival of the fittest, that was what it was all about, both walking wounded racing for the honours in the greatest motor race in the world. So what that most eyes were on the Jags and the Nissans, with both cars now going as fast as their battered condition would allow them Hugh's car was still on schedule to pass the PC

Spice less than two hours from the end.

Six hours to go then five. With the warm summer sun now high in the heavens the heat sapped what strength there was from those who had kept up the night long vigil, the race now being run on adrenalin as much as anything else. And still the Chamberlain car edged closer to its quarry. Five hours to go then four.

A few minutes into his midday stint, de Hennings heart sank as he saw the oil pressure guage take a dive. He was two laps back at the time. A quick pitstop, a thorough check over, there was nothing to be done but put some more in and send him back out.

Standing alone by the pitwall, Hugh Chamberlain watched as Car #128 came past again, the engine sounding rough, its pace almost non-existant. It never returned. Down by the Mulsanne Corner signalling boxes Philippe pulled over and parked it for good.

Hugh Chamberlain had lost out again, having come closer than ever before to gaining that elusive first finish he wants so much. Of course he was bitterly disappointed. Of course he had missed out on a good night's sleep and possibly some valuable drinking time, to boot, though that was the least of his worries. But he never lost his dignity or his will to win, his easy going manner or his long line in quotable quotes.

"We nearly won it though, didn't we! We went out having a go!"

Sunday afternoon and the moment of truth. Hugh Chamberlain turns away from the pitwall after learning of the demise of his Spice's engine. So near yet so far....

SARTHE SNIPPETS

Of the total time frame of twenty-four hours, John Nielsen was at the wheel of the winning car for 12H53, Price Cobb 6H54 and Martin Brundle 4H13. Not belittling the others, the disparity of workload really does go to show what an epic job 'Super John' did, three of his stints extending over two hours each!

This year could have seen the start of the end of an era. While four-times race winner Henri Pescarolo celebrated his twenty-fourth 24 Hours there was no place amongst the driver line-ups for the likes of Claude Ballot-Lena, Jean-Claude Andruet, David Hobbs or Brian Redman, a quartet with no less than seventy-six 'participations' between them. But no victories!

Present only in his capacity as a team owner was Vern Schuppan, his run of sixteen races netting one victory (in 1983) two second places and a third. Although not a pilot himself, the popular Aussie has a fine collection of historic aircraft including a Spitfire and two Mustangs plus a recently acquired ex-Egyptian Air Force YAK-11 fighter/trainer!

Martin Donnelly is now credited with having twice raced at Le Mans – yet on neither occasion has he turned a lap of the event. Last year, the car he was sharing with Blundell and Bailey lasted only a handful of laps, retiring hurt before the Ulsterman had a chance behind the wheel. On this occasion, the car he was sharing with Acheson and Grouillard did not get beyond the parade lap. He was also supposed to run a TWR Jaguar at Daytona'89 only for the car to be eliminated on the second lap, having been started by Derek Daly.

Tim Lee-Davey's purple #19 car was called 'Penny' while its big sister, red #20, was known as 'Petula'. Although both finished, perhaps by the end of a troubled race the ever-optimistic Tim was calling them something else!

Amongst the special tweaks used by Nissan were some special 'soft' gear lever knobs. Organised by team boss Tetsu Ikusawa, the idea was that they enhanced driver comfort. Maybe by next they'll be getting bobbly bead seat backs and sheepskin steering wheel covers too. Bring on the furry dice!

Road car manufacturers are often not much more than designers and assemblers, bodies coming from one sub-contracted source, electrical items another, running gear purchased from a specialist supplier, and so on. Racing is often much the same.

Take the Jaguars, for instance. The chassies are made by ASTEC, a Derbyshire company recently acquired by TWR, the bodywork and doors by John Thompson's enterprise in Northamptonshire. Transmission internals are courtesy of Staffs Gears, brakes from AP. And so it goes on. Even the painting of the cars is done by a company in Nuneaton.

As for Coventry's famous V12, only a semi-machined block is obtained direct from Jaguar, the rest of its mechanical parts being made to specification by Cosworth Engineering.

One-Two-Three is Ich-Ni-San in Japanese. Hence the NISMO lead car always carrying the racing number #23. Not a lot of people know that.

The French Government Tourist Office in London issue some splendid literature about their country. One particular leaflet entitled 'Western Loire' covers the area from St.Nazaire to Tours, Alencon to Poiters. Detailing out the places to go and the things to see thereabouts, under the heading for Le Mans (which is situated in the north-east corner of the region) they draw special attention to the '24 Hours Formula 1 car race'.

How ridiculous; everyone knows that Grand Prix drivers could not remain civil to their team mates for such a long period!

John Colum Crichton-Stuart, Earl of Dumfries, is heir to the sixth Marquis of Bute and therefore (it would appear) almost all the bits of Scotland not owned by either Church or Crown. Interestingly, his inheritance would have been substantially less if his father had been the *younger* of twin brothers. . . .

The Crichton-Stuart family motto is the latin 'Avito Viret Honore' which means 'He Flourishes In An Honourable Ancestry'. Not overly exciting in itself, the translation into Japanese is said by some mechanics to be 'He Crunch 'Em, We Fix 'Em'.

YOU'LL NEVER KNOW HOW MANY FRIENDS YOU HAVE TILL YOU SPONSOR CAR-RACING

FATURBO EXPRESS

David Leslie lives in Cumbria. At a house called 'Bedlam' !

Paul Truswell deserves a standing ovation. In his excellent work for Radio Le Mans for the third successive year he has gone the entire race without having sat down, let alone taken time out to do what comes naturally. He must have a cast iron constitution.

According to the ACO 'Informations Presse' booklet, Jean-Louis Ricci is credited with having the highest number of off-spring of any driver present this year. Four. Fined US$50,000 for signing an absent Bob Wollek on at the Drivers' Briefing, thank goodness that as heir to the 'Nina Ricci' perfume fortune such a silly matter will not affect their pocket money!

Mazdaspeed won the unofficial award for the best Press Pack, their very comprehensive handout containing an abundance of material. Second was the Momo Porsche; not so detailed but very classy. Unfortunately the Silk Cut Jaguar team could not be placed having left a notice in the Press Room stating that if you wanted one you had to go to their compound, knock on the door (it had a spy-hole too) and there it would be decided if you were worthy enough to merit one of their giveaways. Those members of the media with any dignity did not bother.

It is said that The Queen thinks the world smells of new paint, the decorators inevitably preceding her anywhere. Newcomers to Le Mans this year would have been forgiven for thinking that the circuit reminded them of an open sewer. It took the authorities five days to repair a smashed man-hole cover on the roadway adjacent to the lower paddock!

The saga continues. Anyone who has read 'Mercedes Magic – The Story Of The 1989 Le Mans Race' will undoubtably recall the tale of how 1979 race winner Reginald 'Don' Whittington had turned up at a bank with his car boot full of gold bars.

Obviously not one to do things by halves, on 24th January this year he was flying his P–51D Mustang fighter (appropriately nicknamed 'Precious Metal') out west from Florida when he encountered heavy fog in Texas. What is more he was also very low on fuel. Unable to find a suitable landing site before the tank emptied, down went aircraft and pilot and all into the chilly waters of the Gulf of Mexico, about 1½ miles off Galveston.

Whittington was in the sea for nearly two hours before being found by a U S Coast Guard cutter, floating on a seat cushion. Cut and bruised, only semiconscious and suffering from hypothermia, after treatment he recovered well. Unfortunately, the same cannot be said of the Mustang which was all but destroyed in the accident, its remains last seen floating away on the tide to an uncertain fate.

Bearing in mind that Whittington recently served time in prison for drugs related offences – brother and Le Mans co-winner Bill is still there on the same account – there are a number of people who probably wished it had been the other way around. . . .

According to ACO statistics, Rickard Rydell was the youngest driver present, the Schuppan 962 pilot being just 22 last September. The same source indicates a combined age of 78 for the three drivers of the Trust Porsche of Steven Andskar (25) George Fouche (25) and 28-years old Shunji Kasuya.

Last year Kasuya helped win the C2 class. Ironically, one of his co-drivers then, Philippe Farjon, was the oldest participant this time out, the Cougar driver listed as being 54-years old. Others to have passed the magic 'five-o' are Yoshimi Katayama, Gianpiero Moretti and Kumimitsu Takahashi. Senior 'Brit' is Derek Bell, a mere 'enfant' at only 48. . . .

There were other notable absences too. For the first time ever the great French race was run without a French engine taking part, WM Peugeot having upheld Gallic honours in recent seasons, the new 'works' WSPC entry not due to be seen until later in the year.

Also missing from The Great Race this year were the customary 'Patrouille de France' fly-past and the parachutists. Nor were there any Hawaiian Tropic girls. Potentially the most significant of all, there was also a marked absence of British marshalls. Renowned as the best in the world, due to the winter's political machinations only a handful went rather than the normal hundred plus. A sobering indictment. . . .

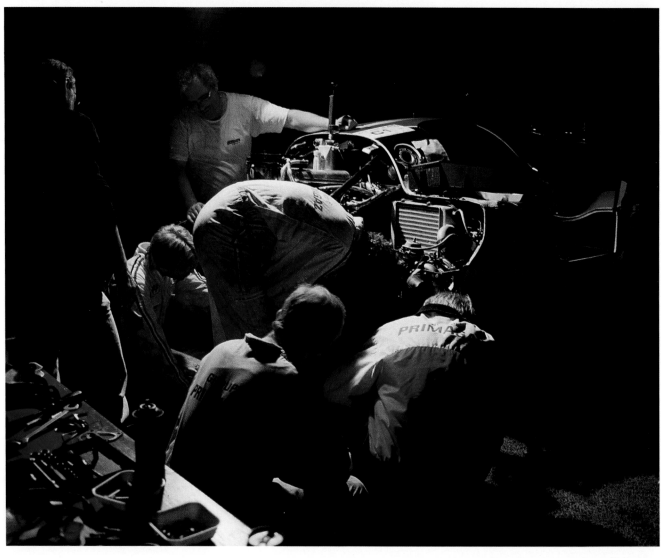

STATISTICS

Position	Driver			Nationality			Number	Team	Main Sponsor(s)	Car Type	Engine
1	Price Cobb	John Nielsen	Martin Brundle	USA	DK	GB	3	TWR	Silk Cut/Castrol	Jaguar XJR12	7.0 Jaguar V12
2	Franz Konrad	Jan Lammers	Andy Wallace	A	NL	GB	2	TWR	Silk Cut/Castrol	Jaguar XJR12	7.0 Jaguar V12
3	Tiff Needell	Anthony Reid	David Sears	GB	GB	GB	45	Alpha	Alpha/Zenitaka	Porsche 962	3.0 Porsche F6t
4	Derek Bell	Frank Jelinski	Hans Stuck	GB	D	D	7	Joest	Blaupunkt	Porsche 962	3.0 Porsche F6t
5	Masahiri Hasemi	Kazu. Hoshino	Toshio Suzuki	J	J	J	23	NISMO	Clasonic	Nissan R89C	3.5 Nissan V8t
6	Geoff Lees	Hitoshi Ogawa	Masanori Sekiya	GB	J	J	36	TOM'S	Minolta	Toyota 90CV	3.2 Toyota V8t
7	Pascal Fabre	Lionel Robert	Michel Trolle	F	F	F	13	Courage	Sarthe/VSD	Cougar C24S	3.0 Porsche F6t
8	Stanley Dickens	'John Winter'	Bob Wollek	S	D	F	9	Joest	Mizuno	Porsche 962	3.0 Porsche F6t
9	Otto Altenbach	Jurgen Laessig	Pierre Yver	D	D	F	27	Obermaier	Primagaz/Dayco	Porsche 962	3.0 Porsche F6t
10	Harald Huysman	Bernard Santal	Massimo Sigala	N	CH	I	15	Brun	Hydro Aluminium	Porsche 962	3.0 Porsche F6t
11	Allen Berg	Bruno Giacomelli	John Watson	CDN	I	GB	44	Lloyd	Italiya	Porsche 962	3.0 Porsche F6t
12	Hurley Haywood	Rickard Rydell	Wayne Taylor	USA	S	GB	33	Schuppan	Takefuji/Yen	Porsche 962	3.0 Porsche F6t
13	Steven Andskar	George Fouche	Shunji Kasuya	S	ZA	J	63	Trust	Nisseki	Porsche 962	3.0 Porsche F6t
14	Jacques Laffite	Henri Pescarolo	J-L Ricci	F	F	F	6	Joest	DB Bank/Primagaz	Porsche 962	3.0 Porsche F6t
15	Thomas Danielsson	Eje Elgh	Tomas Mezera	S	S	AUS	55	Schuppan	Omron	Porsche 962	3.0 Porsche F6t
16	Phillipe Alliot	Bernard de Dryver	Patrick Gonin	F	B	F	11	Kremer	PK/Haute Tension	Porsche 962	3.0 Porsche F6t
17	Bob Earl	Steve Millen	Michael Roe	USA	NZ	IRL	84	NPTI	Unisia	Nissan R90C	3.5 Nissan V8t
18	Tim Harvey	Chris Hodgetts	Fermin Velez	GB	GB	E	21	Spice	Labatts/Raika	Spice SE90C	3.5 Cosworth V8
19	Giovanni Lavaggi	Max Cohen-Olivar		I	MOR		19	Davey	Super Cad/VIP	Porsche 962	3.0 Porsche F6t
20	Yojiro Terada	Yoshimi Katayama	Takashi Yorino	J	J	J	203	Mazda	Charge/Renown	Mazda 767B	1.3 Mazda R4
21	Olindo Iacobelli	Richard Piper	Mike Youles	USA	GB	GB	116	PCA	ATS/Laymead	Spice SE89C	3.3 Cosworth V8
22	Alain Cudini	Costas Los	Hervé Regout	F	GB	B	82	Courage	Simmonds	Nissan R89C	3.5 Nissan V8t
23	J-P Grand	Xavier Lapeyre	M. Maisonneuve	F	F	F	102	Graff	Bouvet Brut/Trilles	Spice SE89C	3.3 Cosworth V8
24	Hideki Okada	Sarel v d Merwe	K. Takahashi	J	ZA	J	10	Kremer	Kenwood	Porsche 962	3.0 Porsche F6t
25	Ross Hyett	James Shead	Robbie Stirling	GB	GB	CDN	103	Mako	Elsafe	Spice SE88C	3.3 Cosworth V8
26	Tim Lee-Davey	Katsunori Iketani		GB	J		20	Davey	Marukatsu/Ross	Porsche 962	3.0 Porsche F6t
27	Stephen Hynes	Richard Jones	Dudley Wood	USA	GB	GB	131	GPM	Bell Group/Olney	Spice SE87C	3.3 Cosworth V8
28	Alistair Fenwick	Alex Postan	Craig Simmiss	GB	GB	NZ	132	GPM	Fenwick/Abbey Life	Tiga GC288	3.3 Cosworth V8
R	Walter Brun	Oscar Larrauri	Jesus Pareja	CH	RA	E	16	Brun	Repsol/FAT	Porsche 962	3.0 Porsche F6t
R	Michel Ferte	Davy Jones	Eliseo Salazar	F	USA	RCH	4	TWR	Silk Cut/Castrol	Jaguar XJR12	7.0 Jaguar V12
R	Robin Donovan	'Charles Hausmann'	P. de Henning	GB	NL	F	128	Chamberl'n	Club Oasis	Spice SE89C	3.3 Cosworth V8
R	Geoff Brabham	Derek Daly	Chip Robinson	AUS	IRL	USA	83	NPTI	Unisia	Nissan R90C	3.5 Nissan V8t
R	Naoki Nagasaki	P-H Raphanel	R. Ratzenberger	J	F	A	38	SARD	Denso	Toyota R90CV	3.2 Toyota V8t
R	Martin Brundle	Alain Ferte	David Leslie	GB	F	GB	1	TWR	Silk Cut/Castrol	Jaguar XJR12	7.0 Jaguar V12
R	Anders Olofsson	M. Sandro-Sala	Takao Wada	S	BR	J	85	TLM	Men's Tenoras	Nissan R89C	3.5 Nissan V8t
R	J J Lehto	Manuel Reuter	James Weaver	SF	D	GB	43	Lloyd	Italiya	Porsche 962	3.0 Porsche F6t
R	F. de Lesseps	P-A Lombardi	Denis Morin	F	F	F	107	Lombardi	GDG/Jouef	Spice SE87C	3.3 Cosworth V8
R	Ian Harrower	Jerry Mahony	John Sheldon	GB	GB	GB	105	ADA	Arquati/Mycil	ADA 03	3.3 Cosworth V8
R	Bertrand Gachot	Johnny Herbert	Volker Weidler	B	GB	D	202	Mazda	Charge/Renown	Mazda 787B	1.3 Mazda R4
R	Pierre Dieudonne	Stefan Johansson	David Kennedy	B	S	IRL	201	Mazda	ART/0123	Mazda 787B	1.3 Mazda R4
R	Julian Bailey	Mark Blundell	G. Brancatelli	GB	GB	I	24	NME	YHP	Nissan R90C	3.5 Nissan V8t
R	Nick Adams	Gunther Gebhardt	Gianpiero Moretti	GB	D	I	230	Gebhardt	Momo	Porsche 962	3.0 Porsche F6t
R	Marc Duez	Harald Grohs	Jurgen Opperman	B	D	D	26	Obermaier	Primagaz/Dayco	Porsche 962	3.0 Porsche F6t
R	Fabio Magnani	Massimo Monti		I	I		54	Mussato	Tauring	Lancia SP90	3.0 Lancia V8t
R	Johnny Dumfries	Roberto Ravaglia	Aguri Suzuki	GB	I	J	37	TOM'S	Taka-Q	Toyota R90CV	3.2 Toyota V8t
R	Alain Ianetta	Pascal Pessiot	Bernard Thuner	F	F	CH	12	Courage	Sarthe/Kofisa	Cougar C24S	3.0 Porsche F6t
R	Phillipe Farjon	Jean Messaoudi		F	F		113	Courage	Chereau	Cougar C20B	2.8 Porsche F6t
R	Jacques Heuclin	Francois Migault	Gerard Tremblay	F	F	F	106	ALD	NRJ/Seine+Marne	ALD C289	3.3 Cosworth V8
NS	Kenny Acheson	Martin Donnelly	Oliver Grouillard	IRL	GB	F	25	NME	JECS	Nissan R90C	3.5 Nissan V8t
NQ	Jonathan Palmer			GB			8	Joest	Blaupunkt	Porsche 962	3.0 Porsche F6t
NQ	Anne Baverey	Micheal Dow	Ian Khan	F	USA	GB	110	Argo	Tamchester	Argo JM19C	3.3 Cosworth V8
NQ	Quirin Bovy	Pancho Egozkue	Pierre de Thoisy	B	E	F	30	GPM	Hipp Sport	Spice SE90C	3.5 Cosworth V8
NQ	Paul Canary	D. Kazmerowski		USA	USA		59	Canary	Eagle Perform.	'Eagle' 700	10.2 Eagle V8
NQ	Noel del Bello	Norbert Santos		F	F		61	ASA	BUT/AFEMP	Norma M6	3.5 MGN W12

DRIVER NOTES :
Jaguar #3 also qualified by Eliseo Salazar (RCH).
Jaguar #4 also qualified by Lius Perez Sala (E).
Lancia #54 also practiced by Andrew Hepworth (GB).

FASTEST LAP :
Steve Millen (Nissan #84)
at 3m40.33 / 138.26 mph
set on Lap 269.

Tyres	Result	Details	Grid Pos	Number	1	2	3	4	5	6	7	8	9	10	11	12	13	14	15	16	17	18	19	20	21	22	23	24
G	359 laps		1 – 3m27.02	24	16	24	24	83	1	1	16	83	83	83	3	3	3	3	3	3	3	3	3	3	3	3	3	3
G	355 laps		2 – 3m33.06	16	24	1	1	1	3	16	4	3	16	3	83	83	83	83	83	16	16	16	16	16	16	16	16	2
Y	352 laps		3 – 3m33.17	23	1	16	83	3	24	83	2	16	3	16	16	2	16	16	16	83	83	7	7	2	2	2	2	45
M	350 laps		4 – 3m33.28	83	3	83	3	16	4	4	3	2	2	2	2	16	2	23	23	7	7	2	2	7	45	45	45	7
BD	348 laps		5 – 3m35.76	25	83	3	2	4	23	3	83	4	23	23	23	23	23	1	1	2	2	45	23	45	23	23	23	23
B	347 laps		6 – 3m36.08	7	2	2	4	24	83	2	24	24	7	7	4	4	1	7	7	45	23	23	45	23	7	7	7	36
G	347 laps		7 – 3m36.10	4	4	4	16	2	16	24	23	23	45	4	1	1	7	2	2	9	45	9	9	36	36	36	36	13
M	346 laps		8 – 3m36.55	1	23	23	23	45	2	7	45	45	4	1	7	7	45	45	45	23	9	13	36	9	9	13	13	9
G	341 laps		9 – 3m37.00	3	9	9	45	7	9	23	7	7	9	45	45	45	9	9	9	4	4	36	13	13	13	9	9	27
Y	335 laps		10 – 3m37.13	36	43	45	9	23	45	45	9	9	1	9	9	9	4	4	4	36	36	27	27	27	27	27	27	15
G	335 laps		11 – 3m38.28	63	36	43	10	9	7	6	6	6	1	24	33	33	36	36	36	13	13	15	4	4	15	15	15	44
D	332 laps		12 – 3m38.39	10	37	10	43	33	37	9	1	6	6	36	36	13	33	13	13	27	27	4	15	15	44	44	44	33
D	330 laps		13 – 3m38.72	43	10	44	7	13	6	13	13	33	33	6	13	33	13	6	27	15	15	83	44	44	33	33	33	63
G	328 laps		14 – 3m38.74	37	44	7	6	55	13	27	33	13	13	13	6	6	6	27	15	11	44	44	11	11	36	63	63	6
D	326 laps		15 – 3m39.38	26	45	82	36	6	55	33	27	27	36	27	27	27	27	15	63	44	11	11	33	33	6	6	6	55
Y	319 laps		16 – 3m39.76	38	7	37	33	43	33	36	36	36	27	24	43	43	43	33	44	63	63	63	63	63	55	55	55	11
G	311 laps		17 – 3m39.78	2	33	33	13	36	43	43	43	43	43	26	15	15	15	63	6	82	38	33	6	6	11	11	11	84
G	308 laps		18 – 3m40.01	9	6	6	55	27	36	203	230	26	26	43	63	55	55	44	11	38	33	6	55	55	10	84	84	21
D	306 laps		19 – 3m40.27	11	85	13	37	230	21	230	26	15	230	15	38	63	63	38	38	33	82	38	83	10	84	21	21	20
D	304 laps		20 – 3m41.32	45	26	55	203	203	201	11	15	230	203	230	55	38	44	11	82	6	6	82	10	84	20	116	116	203
G	304 laps		21 – 3m42.73	44	84	15	26	11	26	85	85	203	15	201	201	44	38	82	33	55	55	55	84	20	21	20	20	116
G	300 laps		22 – 3m43.04	202	82	21	21	201	27	26	82	85	201	21	44	85	85	203	203	203	10	10	20	116	116	10	203	82
G	291 laps		23 – 3m43.35	201	11	11	201	82	203	82	203	82	85	63	85	11	11	85	55	10	21	84	82	21	203	203	82	192
Y	279 laps		24 – 3m43.40	85	13	36	27	85	230	15	201	201	21	38	11	82	82	55	116	116	84	20	21	128	82	82	102	10
G	274 laps		25 – 3m44.28	84	15	203	230	26	82	201	11	21	63	44	82	203	203	116	10	21	20	21	116	82	102	102	10	103
D	260 laps		26 – 3m44.34	13	55	202	44	15	11	107	21	63	55	55	203	116	116	10	21	84	116	116	128	203	103	103	103	19
G	259 laps		27 – 3m45.44	33	203	26	12	21	12	102	63	44	44	85	24	20	10	21	84	20	128	128	203	102	19	19	19	131
A	254 laps		28 – 3m45.57	27	21	230	82	107	44	21	116	55	38	11	128	10	21	20	20	128	203	203	102	103	132	131	131	132
Y	353 laps	Engine	29 – 3m45.66	82	202	27	84	102	85	44	44	116	82	203	116	128	20	84	128	102	102	102	103	19	131	132	132	
G	282 laps	Engine	30 – 3m45.77	6	63	201	11	116	15	116	55	38	11	82	21	105	84	128	102	103	103	19	131					
G	254 laps	Engine	31 – 3m46.03	55	201	12	107	63	107	63	107	11	116	116	20	21	128	102	19	19	19	132	131					
G	251 laps	Fuel Leak	32 – 3m47.75	21	230	107	102	44	102	20	20	10	128	128	202	84	107	105	107	132	132	132	131					
D	241 laps	Engine	33 – 3m47.92	15	107	128	116	105	116	55	38	128	202	202	10	26	105	103	19	131	131	131						
G	220 laps	Water Pump	34 – 3m49.45	203	20	84	105	128	105	38	10	202	20	20	105	107	19	102	132									
Y	182 laps	Electrics	35 – 3m49.96	230	128	102	15	20	84	10	102	20	105	105	84	202	103	19	131									
G	181 laps	Tyre/Fire	36 – 3m50.69	103	27	131	20	37	63	202	128	105	103	10	107	19	102	202										
G	170 laps	Accident	37 – 3m54.56	54	12	116	128	38	202	105	202	103	10	107	19	103	202	131										
G	164 laps	Suspension	38 – 3m57.49	107	102	20	85	10	128	128	103	107	107	84	103	102	131	132										
D	148 laps	Electrics	39 – 3m59.34	102	116	19	113	202	20	103	105	102	84	103	102	131	132											
D	147 laps	Engine	40 – 3m59.54	12	131	63	202	103	10	54	54	84	19	19	131	132												
D	142 laps	Engine	41 – 4m00.07	19	38	113	63	12	38	131	19	19	131	102	132													
G	138 laps	Gearbox	42 – 4m00.55	113	113	105	38	54	103	132	84	54	102	131														
G	130 laps	Gearbox	43 – 4m02.59	131	105	85	103	131	113	19	131	132	132	132														
D	86 laps	Accident	44 – 4m03.03	106	106	106	131	84	54	84	132	131																
D	64 laps	Accident	45 – 4m04.09	128	54	103	132	132	132																			
G	57 laps	Engine	46 – 4m04.73	116	19	38	19	19	131																			
G	43 laps	Accident	47 – 4m10.46	132	103	132	54	113	106																			
D	36 laps	Gearbox	48 – 4m13.64	105	132	54	106	106	19																			
D	DNS	Gearbox	49 – 4m14.90	20																								
M	DNQ	Accident	50 – 3m43.79	8																								
G	DNQ	Engine	51 – 4m17.79	110																								
D	DNQ	Engine	52 – 4m20.93	30																								
G	DNQ	Engine	53 – 5m39.02	59																								
A	DNQ	Engine	54 – NO TIME	61																								

TYRES :
A = Avon
B = Bridgestone
D = Dunlop
G = Goodyear
M = Michelin
Y = Yokohama

REVISED CIRCUIT LENGTH :
13.60 kms / 8.45 miles.

MERCEDES *Magic*

THE STORY OF THE 1989 LE MANS RACE

KEN WELLS

1989 marked a very special year in the history of the Le Mans 24 Hours, the year the Silver Arrows found their target.

'Mercedes Magic' relives the story of that epic success in glorious style!

Written by Ken Wells, this 128-page book includes features on Daytona, the early WSPC rounds, the whole story of Le Mans qualifying and race, how a C2 team fared, Hawaiian Tropic girls and all the fun of the fair!

With additional words by John Allen and Mike Cotton, there are interviews with winner Jochen Mass, TWR boss Tom Walkinshaw, Jaguar driver Andrew Gilbert-Scott, the mercurial Hans Stuck and Spice designer Graham Humphrys. And much more besides.

An ideal reference source for modellers, 'Mercedes Magic' contains over 200 superb ALL COLOUR photographs (including every car present) by such notables as Jeff Bloxham and Malcolm Bryan while the airbrush illustrations by Rosemary Hutchings are worth the cover price alone!

Copies can be obtained direct from the author at 4, Highfield Rise, Althorne, Essex, CM36DN at the special reduced price of £9–95 while stocks last.

Please add £2–50 for UK or £5–00 for overseas postage, making cheques/IMOs/postal orders payable to Prancing Tortoise Publications. Sorry, no foreign currencies or credit cards.